Margaret Attwood is Manager of Organizational Development for the Mid Essex Health Authority. Prior to this she was Principal Lecturer in Personnel Management and Industrial Relations in the Department of General Management, North East London Polytechnic (formerly Anglian Regional Management Centre). She has undertaken a wide range of lecturing and consultancy assignments. A major interest is the development and implementation of equal opportunity policies. She is a member of the panel of independent experts designated by the Advisory, Conciliation and Arbitration Service to deal with equal value cases and also of the Postgraduate Courses Board of the Council for National Academic Awards.

PAN MANAGEMENT GUIDES

Other books in the series:

Advertising and PR
Company Accounts
Financial Management
Industrial Relations
Management Accounting
Marketing
Production and Operations Management

PAN MANAGEMENT GUIDES

Personnel Management

Margaret Attwood

Pan Original
Pan Books London and Sydney

First published 1987 by Pan Books Ltd,
Cavaye Place, London SW10 9PG
9 8 7 6 5 4 3 2 1
© Margaret Attwood 1987
ISBN 0 330 29366 4
Photoset by Parker Typesetting Service, Leicester
Printed and bound in Great Britain by
Hazell Watson & Viney Limited,
Member of the BPCC Group,
Aylesbury, Bucks

Contents

Introduction   7

1 Definitions of Personnel Management   9
2 Recruitment and Selection   17
3 The Law and the Rights of the New Employee   40
4 Employee Involvement   51
5 Appraising Performance   65
6 Training for Current Jobs   74
7 Developing People for the Future   91
8 Looking After Employees – Welfare and
   Counselling Services   100
9 The Law and the Rights of the Individual
   Employee   108
10 Fair Pay and Employee Benefits at Work   120
11 Dismissal, Redundancy and Retirement   142

Introduction

This book is about the search for success in organizations through the effective use of people. Unfortunately, in the past, more attention has been given to the mismanagement of employees and the reasons for this than to the development of criteria for success in personnel management. Any attempt to generate universal prescriptions for effectiveness in this area of management practice is likely to be misleading. What appears to encourage work of both high quality and quantity in one organization may not have the same result elsewhere. Nor should we assume that other nations have all the answers. At one time everything American was thought likely to lead to industrial utopia. Now many people are excited by Japanese management techniques. This guide examines the process of managing people at work as practised by personnel specialists, supervisors and line managers. It does not pretend to be a panacea for all ills. Rather it is an attempt to encourage readers to make the effort to examine the circumstances of their own organizations. On the basis of such an analysis it is possible to develop policies, strategies and practices for managing employees, which will work best there. In this way it should assist the acquisition of relevant knowledge by new entrants to these occupations as well as providing some 'food for thought' for those already established in such positions. I hope that it will encourage a recognition of the complexity of good personnel management, a rejection of easy solutions and a stimulation to further reading and questioning, where relevant, of existing employment practices.

While writing this guide, I have learnt the difficulty of attempting to compress a large area of knowledge into a small amount of text. Of necessity I have made decisions about the emphasis which should be given to particular aspects of the subject. Without doubt this reflects my own experience and values.

Those who have wittingly or unwittingly helped me to acquire the knowledge on which this guide is based are too numerous to mention. However, in particular, I should like to thank many of my erstwhile colleagues especially Win Stenning and Patrick Hare at the Anglian Regional Management Centre, North East London Polytechnic and those personnel practitioners with whom I have had contact over the years. Also, without the support of Bill, Abi and Jonathan there would have been no book at all.

1 Definitions of Personnel Management

Personnel management is concerned with the management of people at work. A general summary of the characteristics of personnel management practice would be along the following lines:

- a wide range of people – personnel specialists, line managers and supervisors – practice personnel management
- most organizations have a specialist personnel department which gives support to managers and supervisors, who have direct responsibility for the management of people
- there are several specialist management techniques which together comprise personnel management
- the practice of personnel management varies greatly from one organization to another.

1 Universal Good Practice in Personnel Management?

The central concern of personnel management is the efficient use of one of the resources available to organizations – its employees. In this way, it can be equated with other functions of management – finance, production or marketing. Unfortunately, although there are books which purport to provide answers to all 'people management' problems, there is little universal 'good practice' in this area of management. Techniques which appear to assist in the effective utilization of manpower in one organization may fail elsewhere. For example, where a company has a history of strikes, employees may react with hostility to managerial proposals on new working practices; where industrial peace has been the norm for years, and relationships between management and workers have been good, there probably would be much less distrust of identical proposals. No universal principles govern the formulation of personnel policies and techniques. However, there are certain basic headings and guidelines which together comprise personnel management. For example, the Institute of Personnel Management says personnel is that part of the management process concerned with:

- recruiting and selecting people
- training and developing them for their work
- ensuring that their payment and conditions of employment are appropriate, where necessary negotiating such terms of employment with trade unions
- advising on healthy and appropriate conditions
- monitoring the organization of people at work
- encouraging good relations between management and work people.

In other words, no matter what the organizational context, it is always necessary for someone to have responsibility for the movement of people into, through and out of an organization, if the human resource is to be effectively managed. However, the detailed organization of such responsibilities, for example by managers or supervisors and specialists, and the specific techniques employed will differ from organization to organization.

Personnel Policy Formulation

There are no general prescriptions for the creation of good relations with employees. Therefore, managers and personnel specialists can use their knowledge and skills successfully only if they are based on a broad understanding of the nature of and influences on the employment relationship in their own organization. Management's general objectives are predominantly financial. Hence, in this area management is concerned to keep down the cost of employing people whilst at the same time achieving the highest productivity. The means of achieving this end will differ from organization to organization, depending upon the values held by senior management about the management of people at work. It is helpful to the pursuit of effectiveness in personnel management if there is a written or at least a well-understood set of principles to guide all managers in their dealings with employees. In many organizations, little thought has been given to the explicit formulation of personnel policies. The employee relations implications of corporate decision making are often examined after financial, production or marketing plans have been made. However there are benefits in considering personnel management as a facet of corporate decision making.

Suppose a frozen food manufacturer decides to expand. Two options are identified – the acquisition of a chain of freezer centres or the opening of another frozen food factory. Clearly, the financial, marketing and operational implications of both options must be analysed in detail. However, the human resource implications should be considered also. For example, if the food manufacturing company has had a history of poor employee relations, the better option might be acquisition of the retail chain. Small workplaces are less conflict ridden than large ones. Strikes are less frequent in the private services sector of British industry than in manufacturing. This would not guarantee industrial peace but would suggest that this could be achieved with goodwill on both sides. On the other hand, if relations with employees in the food manufacturing company were good and productivity was high, the least risky expansion strategy from the personnel management standpoint might be to open another similar factory. An additional influence on such a decision might be the number of managers and technologists with potential for better jobs, who would be available for work in the new factory.

It is not only expanding organizations which should take care to formulate personnel policies. Management everywhere should assess its effectiveness in personnel management periodically and establish whether change in policies or practice is necessary. Effective management of employees requires foresight, planning and the commitment of top management.

2 Planning for People in Organizations

Effectiveness in personnel management requires not only effective policy formulation but also planned policy implementation. Human resource planning involves the identification and analysis of factors influencing the future demand for, and supply of, labour.

Examples of both influences on a manufacturing company are listed below.

Factors Influencing the Demand for Labour

- The objectives of the company and its future plans
- Market demand for the company's products
- The technology used by the company
- The product range or numbers of models produced
- The productivity per employee
- The degree to which components are 'bought in'
- The level of stock

Factors Influencing the Supply of Labour

- Company policies in so far as they affect recruitment and selection, manning levels, retirement and redundancy
- The attractiveness of jobs in the company, including pay and other terms and conditions of employment
- The skills available in the labour market
- Union agreements, for example on manning levels
- Government legislation, for example on employees' rights

The planning of human resources, then, involves trying to obtain:

- the right people
- in the right numbers
- with the right knowledge, skills and experience
- in the right jobs
- in the right place
- at the right time
- at the right cost

It can be seen as an attempt to balance the demand for employees with the numbers available. However, it is not merely a 'numbers exercise' concerned with the QUANTITY of manpower; it also involves issues related to the QUALITY of manpower, such as the requirements for training and development.

A well designed human resource plan provides a clear framework for day-to-day effective personnel management.

3 Who Practises Personnel Management?

The Institute of Personnel Management stresses that personnel management 'forms part of every manager's job as well as being the particular concern of the specialist'.

Personnel Roles and Responsibilities

In practice, the specialist role may take a number of forms:

- executive
- facilitator
- consultancy
- service
- audit

The Executive Role

Personnel management is part of every manager's job, but some personnel activities are carried out by specialists rather than by line managers or supervisors. Factors which seem to influence the division of responsibilities include potential economies of scale if the activity is carried out by specialists, the need for 'expert' knowledge, organizational tradition, and the preferences of both specialists and line managers. For example, personnel specialists tend to maintain a high profile in those areas of work which they see as most important and prestigious. Industrial relations falls into this category.

The Faciliator Role

Many personnel management activities require considerable skills and knowledge if they are to be carried out effectively. One of the responsibilities of personnel specialists is to see that those who practise such activities, as part of a more general managerial role, are equipped to do so. Attempts by personnel practitioners to carry out this task may lead to conflict between themselves and line managers. For example, the latter may resist efforts to increase their effectiveness in performance appraisal interviewing.

The Consultancy Role

Managers may confront a variety of problems as they attempt to supervise employees. These may include motivation difficulties, lack of training or pay grievances. The individual manager may meet a particular problem infrequently and, therefore, may need advice to resolve it successfully. In this area, the role of the personnel specialist can be equated with that of an internal management consultant.

The Service Role

Managers need information on which to base decisions about deployment of their staff. The personnel specialist can provide, for example, statistics on pay nationally, by industry or by occupation. Because of the increased complexity of employment legislation, there is often a need for information on interpretation of such laws by the courts as well as the detail of the law itself.

The Audit Role

Personnel specialists have responsibility for ensuring that all members of management carry out those parts of their jobs relating to effective use of human resources.

This categorization of the work of the personnel specialist is not definitive. There wll be overlap between roles. For example, in the area of advice on employment legislation, there will often be little distinction between 'service' and 'consultancy'. At times, one role will assume greater significance at the expense of others; for example, in a recession, pressure on indirect costs, of which a personnel department is one, may restrict the more creative aspects of the work of specialists – the 'facilitator' and 'consultancy' roles. It is wrong to assume that personnel specialists should operate always in one particular way. Far better that those involved recognize the potential variations in the role and can diagnose the optimum division of labour between specialists and line managers.

The Personnel Role of the Line Manager

All managers should recognize the need to be effective in handling those whom they supervise. Far too frequently, selection for managerial jobs is based on an assessment of professional or technical competence in previous jobs rather than skills in the management of people or the potential to develop these. This book is written to help all concerned with this difficult aspect of management. However, certain core skills and orientations for effective human resource management can be identified:

- the need to identify one's own perspective on the employment relationship and that of other people
- an ability to recognize that employees may have different objectives from those of management
- a recognition of the need for personnel policies compatible with the needs of the business, to which all members of management are committed
- a commitment to personal development in all relevant aspects of personnel management
- an awareness of one's limitations in this area and a willingness to seek specialist help where necessary.

2 Recruitment and Selection

This chapter considers the process of matching the characteristics of individuals to the demands of jobs. This is the purpose of recruitment and selection. As in other areas of personnel management, you will find that, unfortunately, there are no easy prescriptions for success. Much depends on the knowledge and skills of those involved, whether line managers or personnel specialists. In addition, any personnel technique needs to be relevant to, and effective within, the context of a particular organization.

1 How to start

When considering staff recruitment managers should ask themselves several questions:

- what job do I want to be done?
- what kind of person do I think will do it most effectively?
- how can I find some people who might be suitable to fill the job?
- what methods should I use to decide which one would best fit my requirements?

In summary, the recruitment and selection process can be seen as a number of stages:

- defining the job to be done
- defining the characteristics of the ideal candidate
- attracting candidates
- selecting candidates.

Many people think this is a simple process. After all with

many people unemployed, managers should have no difficulty in filling vacancies. If currently you are involved in recruitment, you will know that the difficulties lie not in attracting candidates, but in choosing the most suitable from large numbers of candidates.

In the 1930s, when queues of unemployed people waited at the factory gates for work, foremen would come and choose 'you, you and you'. Since then, recruitment and selection techniques have developed to give a better basis for decision-making. However, predictions about other people are subject to error. All recruiters make mistakes. Recruitment is more of an art than a science but, systematically planned, there should be less risk that you place 'square pegs in round holes'.

2 Stage One: Defining the job to be done

This stage of the recruitment and selection process can be thus summarized:

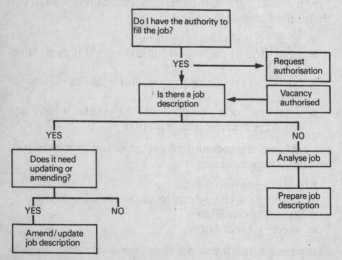

Figure 1. Defining the job to be done

When an employee leaves a job there is an opportunity to assess whether the job needs to be done at all or whether the work could be reorganized.

Job Analysis

The tasks which the job comprises must be analysed. The main steps involved are:

- identifying the tasks involved in the job
- examining how, when and why tasks are performed
- noting the physical, social and financial conditions of the job.

From this information a job description should be written. This is vital to the success of the rest of the recruitment and selection process. It is the basic building block on which advertising, interviewing and other processes are constructed. An effective job description should describe:

- the job
- its place in the organization
- the circumstances in which it is performed
- the objectives to be achieved by the job holder

and it should be:

- a useful working document
- up-to-date and relevant
- concise but comprehensive in its coverage of the demands of the job.

3 Stage Two: Defining the ideal candidate

Having prepared a job description for the vacancy under consideration, we now need to match the characteristics of the job with the characteristics of candidates who may apply. To undertake this process satisfactorily, we need a picture of the ideal candidate. Such a picture is called a 'person specification'.

Many human attributes can be stipulated as requirements for the performance of jobs. It is usual to list the requirements under suitable headings. Below is the system most commonly used:

The 'Seven Point Plan'

1 **Physical make-up** – health, appearance, bearing and speech
2 **Attainments** – education, qualifications, experience
3 **General intelligence** – intellectual capacity
4 **Special aptitudes** – mechanical, manual dexterity, facility in use of words and figures
5 **Interests** – intellectual, practical, constructional, physically active, social, artistic
6 **Disposition** – acceptability, influence over others, steadiness, dependability, self-reliance
7 **Circumstances** – any special demands of the job, such as ability to work unsocial hours, travel abroad, etc.

In drawing up personnel specifications, managers should take care that selection criteria are not unlawfully discriminatory. (See Chapter 3 pages 43–47.) The best way to avoid trouble is to ensure that all attributes listed in a personnel specification are directly related to the demands of the job. The 'circumstances' heading of the Seven Point Plan could be discriminatory against women, if managers list there that applicants must be single or must not have small children. It is much fairer to state that applicants must be able to work 'unsocial' or long hours if work demands this.

The aim of a personnel specification is to set a standard against which all candidates can be judged. It may be difficult to find the ideal candidate. For this reason, it is usual to write personnel specifications under two headings 'essential' and 'desirable'. This allows managers to adjust the yardstick against which to judge candidates in light of changing labour market conditions.

4 Stage Three: Attracting Candidates

Having written a personnel specification, it is necessary to encourage some people to become applicants. Possible sources of applicants for jobs are:

- internal advertisements or analysis of personnel records
- external advertisements
- employment agencies – private or public
- schools, colleges or other institutions providing training courses
- casual callers or writers of letters
- recommendations from existing employees.

Advertisements

Over 4000 publications in the United Kingdom carry recruitment advertisements. As well as the written word, employers use radio, television and computerized information systems such as Oracle and Prestel. We shall not examine each of these in detail. We are concerned with the principles of effective recruitment advertising. These can be established by answering the following questions:

- Where am I likely to find potential candidates?

You need to know where candidates are likely to be currently working or undergoing education or training and where they live. Some candidates can be found in the local labour market, because their skills can be used by many employers; those who occupy specialist positions are part of a national labour market. There would be little point in a local solicitor advertising for a typist in a national newspaper!

■ How can I attract them to work for me?

To answer this question you need to think about what would attract a candidate to the job.
These include:

■ Earnings (including any bonus)
■ Perks, e.g. discount on goods, overalls, canteen, other staff facilities
■ Hours of work
■ Holidays
■ Company name, size, location etc.
■ Conditions of work, rush hours, quiet times
■ Training
■ Promotion prospects
■ Job security
■ Notice periods.

Designing a recruitment advertisement is a marketing exercise, in which the preferences of potential candidates should be compared with the features of the job (taken from the job description). Those aspects which are most likely to appeal can be emphasized. If there are significant problems in recruiting candidates who meet the requirements of the personnel specification, you may wish to consider specific advantages and disadvantages of the job to identify the selling points.

It is also useful to ensure that a recruitment advertisement contains a brief profile of the ideal applicant, drawn from the personnel specification. This should cut out some of the wasted effort involved in responding to a vast number of applicants, most of whom are marginal or unsuitable.

Effective advertisements should have:

- A compelling headline
- Interesting content
- Clear, unambiguous information about the job and the likely candidate
- Information on how to apply
- Eye-catching design and typography.

External Recruitment Agencies

Several options are open to organizations which choose an external agency for recruitment purposes:

- Government agencies – in the United Kingdom, the Job Centre or Professional and Executive register (PER)
- Private employment agencies
- Selection consultants who provide a shortlist of candidates
- Executive search consultants or 'head-hunters', who will contact suitable candidates direct
- Advertising agencies which design and place advertisements
- A combination of these.

Some options can be expensive. Selection consultants can charge up to 20 per cent of the annual salary of the job to be filled.

In choosing a recruitment channel or source of applicants you should reflect on your past experience and consider:

- the audience to be reached
- the nature of the job
- the desired image of the employing organization
- cost effectiveness
- time required to fill the vacancy.

5 Stage Four: Selecting Candidates

The following flow chart below summarizes the main stages of the selection process from receiving applications to making an appointment.

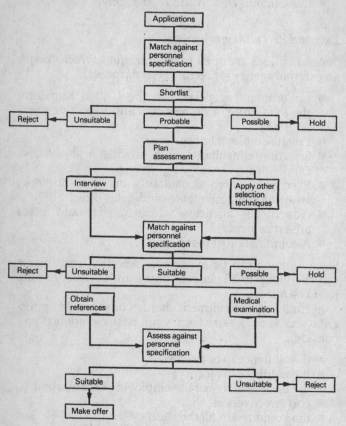

Figure 2. Flow chart of the selection process

Variations from this are possible depending on the requirements of the organization. For example, medical examination may be used for older applicants, where jobs are particularly physically demanding and where safety is vital (e.g. airline pilots). In other cases medical history questionnaires are often sufficient.

The employer's objectives in the selection process are:

- To appoint the right person for the job
- To establish or maintain an image as a good employer
- To make the process as cost effective as possible.

It is useful to encourage an element of self-selection by sending applicants 'further details', consisting of information about the organization, the job and the ideal candidate. Some applicants may withdraw after matching their characteristics against the requirements of the job.

Shortlisting

For many jobs it is possible to eliminate most candidates without seeing them. Letters of application, curricula vitae, and, above all, application forms can be used as screening devices. Letters of application and cvs are less likely to be vague, if the advertisement is specific about the nature of the job and the person required to perform it. Nevertheless, there are usually more problems in matching information thus received from applicants than if it is presented on a well-designed application form. For more senior jobs, it is quite common to require candidates to make a self-assessment of their suitability.

Interviewing

Research has cast doubt on both the validity and

reliability of the selection interview. Validity is how well the assessment procedure predicts future successful job performance; reliability is the degree to which the same or different interviewers would reach the same selection decision. We would have little confidence in a thermometer which gave different readings in boiling water on different days! If something is not reliable, it cannot be valid. However, surveys show that almost all organizations use the interview as a means of selection. This is because:

- Interviewing may be cheaper than other selection methods, especially tests
- The interview allows candidates to obtain information about the job and the organization as well as providing a medium through which they may be judged by the interviewer
- After the interview candidates should feel that they have had a fair deal from the organization
- If the interview is conducted by the person to whom the new employee would report, it allows the parties to assess their mutual compatibility.

Whatever the interview's validity or reliability most employers will continue to use it. Probably the best way to proceed is to use trained interviewers who are aware of the problems inherent in the process.

The Halo Effect and Interviewer Bias

If you ever have to interview someone with the same educational or work background as yourself, beware! There is a tendency in all of us to recruit in our own 'image'. You may assume that, because the candidate shares some aspect of your background or interests, he or she must share your characteristics as a bright successful human being! Really? It is rumoured that junior doctors in teaching hospitals often are selected more for their rugby prowess than for their medical skills. The 'old boy' network operates similarly – one of the reasons why women find it difficult to break into the upper echelons.

Similarly, if you feel early in the interview that the candidate marries up well to the requirements of the job, you may well allow this 'halo' to cloud your judgement during the rest of the interview.

Interviewer bias or prejudice sometimes may be based on physical characteristics. Some people dislike people with beards or long hair.

Such psychological processes make it likely that the interviewer decides for or against a candidate in the opening minutes of the interview. The rest of the time is then spent trying to prove first impressions accurate.

The Need for Systematic Preparation

Interviewers must be well informed about both the job description and the personnel specification. They should brief themselves adequately about candidates. A well designed application form is vital here. Preparation should go beyond being able to read candidates' own words back to them from the application form! This is likely to frustrate applicants.

Questioning Techniques

'Effective interviewers ask good questions.' This is one of the most important interviewing skills.

Open Questions

One of the key purposes of selection interviewing is to elicit information to allow the candidate's characteristics to be matched against the requirements laid down in the personnel specification.

'Why did you apply for this job?'
'Why did you choose that course?'

Closed Questions

These are questions to which the only answer can be, 'Yes', 'No' or 'I don't know'. They may be used to check information or to get a definite response quickly. Effective interviewers ensure their use is restricted. An interview which relies heavily on these is rather wooden. A further danger is that such questions may push the candidate into false polarizations. For example the question:

'Did you enjoy your college course?'

may provoke the answer, 'Yes', where the reality could be more complex. More garrulous or helpful candidates may expand the answer without prompting but the interviewer should be aware that control of the interview is being relinquished.

Probing Questions

Sometimes the candidate's answers will lack depth or clarity.

'I left that job because I felt the career prospects were nonexistent.'

A probing question following this might be:

'Why do you say that?'
'What kind of career development did you want?'

Sometimes the response to such a question will be slow. The interviewer should not rephrase the question or help the candidate in any other way. The time taken to reply probably indicates that it is an effective probing question.

Multiple Questions

If the interviewer had asked both my probing questions at the same time this would have been a multiple question. These are faulty since the candidate can choose which question to answer. Again the interviewer is in danger of surrendering control of the situation.

Linking Questions or Statements

An interview should be a conversation with a purpose. One useful way of achieving this aim is for the interviewer to indicate, after completing a particular area of questioning, that it is time to look at another topic.

'Now that we've discussed your work experience, can we have a look at your activities outside work?'

Leading Questions

These should be avoided in selection interviews since they are likely to feed the interviewer's own prejudices and desire to confirm early impressions.

'We are anxious to appoint someone who is good at dealing with the public. You'd be all right there, wouldn't you?'

What fool is going to deny this?

Problem-centred Questions

You may wish to gain an impression of the likely response of the candidate to particular situations.

'Could you tell me about the most difficult customer you had to deal with, when you were doing that Saturday job?'

Such questions are very useful if relevant to the job in

question and they can realistically be answered by the interviewee.

Discriminatory Questions

These are illegal under anti-discrimination legislation (see Chapter 3) since they indicate an intention to discriminate on grounds of sex, marital status or race. Managers should ensure that all questions are job related:

> 'Are the hours required by this job likely to cause you any problems?'

Indirect Questions

If candidates are asked, 'Do you get on with other people?' control of the interview is being passed to the interviewee. It is probably better to ask about relationships with fellow workers or friends or for information on behaviour in particular circumstances. The interviewer can judge the applicants' relationships with others.

Stress Interviews

Such situations attempt to simulate the stress generated by the job to assess whether the candidate would cope. Some interviews for managerial positions are structured in this way. The problems of validity and reliability discussed earlier make me sceptical about this approach. Indeed, with some candidates, they may be counterproductive. A friend of mine was shown into an office for an interview. Behind a desk sat a man obscured from sight by the newspaper he was reading. My friend waited. Presumably there was an attempt to create stress by the ambiguity of the situation. My friend was immensely irritated and left. Would he have been suitable for the job? Could an interviewer make an accurate judgement from his reaction to this situation? I doubt it!

Interview Structure

Many experienced interviewers say they have difficulty in ensuring that they always cover all relevant ground during an interview. A check list based on the headings of the personnel specification is helpful. This may form a basis for the interview structure. Details about the job can be given after obtaining information about the candidate. This avoids the necessity of giving details to obviously unsuitable candidates. Time should be allowed for questions from the candidate.

Panel Interviews

In the public sector, in the United Kingdom, it is common to use panel interviews where a candidate faces several interviewers at once. Opinions differ as to whether these are more or less valid than one to one interviews. Broadly, the following principles should be observed:

- All participants should have a genuine claim to be involved
- All interviewers should be skilled and experienced
- Proper planning and coordination is vital
- It is probably better to use a 'tight' structure, where each interviewer takes a particular role and a chairman acts as a coordinator.

The Don'ts of Interviewing

Interviewers should not:

- keep the interviewee waiting
- interview without systematic preparation and planning
- allow the interview to be interrupted
- ask trick, leading, multiple or discriminatory questions or too many closed questions

- lose control of the interview to the interviewee
- fail to give the candidate information about the job
- take copious notes during the interview
- display bias or prejudice
- talk too much (probably not more than one third of the interview time)
- allow the candidate to gloss over important points.

This list is not exhaustive and some of the points overlap.

Selection Testing

Selection tests are used to provide a standardized, reliable, objective measure of applicants' skills. There are two main types:

- Tests of capacity
- Tests of personality and attitudes

Tests of Capacity

The aim is to match the individual's abilities to various job requirements. Some jobs require the use of specialist skills. For example, aptitude tests have been devised to test the capacity of potential computer programmers. Other tests of capacity may be more general. For example, many tests concern mental ability. Postmen are tested for literacy, powers of observation, speed in perception and in checking information and short term memory ability to translate a code into comprehensible instructions. Another well known group of tests aims to measure general mental ability or intelligence. This can be defined as the ability to learn and to use learning to reason. Such tests are often used for graduate entrants. Manual dexterity tests are used in the clothing industry to test how quickly and accurately a simple assembly task can be carried out.

Tests of Personality and Attitude

These fall into two categories:

- Questionnaires (usually multiple choice paper and pencil tests)
- Projective techniques (where candidates are asked to project themselves into the test situation).

Validation of Tests

Tests should have been validated for use with particular occupational groups. In other words it should have been possible to show that high performers on the test are the most successful in job performance and vice versa for low test performers. Recent surveys suggest that significant numbers of employers do not attempt to validate the tests they use. Tests must be validated for three reasons:

- To ensure they are able to predict job success
- To show how fairly the test samples the knowledge which trainees or job holders should have mastered
- To assess how far the test is consistent with the attributes it purports to measure. (For example, tests of leadership should be capable of measuring leadership traits and leadership should be vital to effective job performance.)

Some people argue that selection tests may be biased against minority groups.

It may be advantageous to use selection tests:

- As part of a selection procedure, when large numbers of people must be recruited
- When it is impossible to rely on educational qualifications as a predictor of job success
- When sufficient time is available to validate the

tests on the particular occupational group for which the test has been designed.

References

This is fraught with problems. Applicants are unlikely to name referees who will indicate their unsuitability for a job. Some people suggest, for this reason, that references from a previous employer, who is less likely to gloss over the problem areas, should be used. Will this always be so? Probably not. Some employers will simply lack awareness of the job. Hence they may give an unhelpful or misleading reference quite unwittingly. The more unscrupulous may deliberately mislead, either by writing a glowing reference about an employee they wish to lose, or an unfavourable one about an employee they wish to retain.

References can be made more reliable by:

- asking a previous employer for factual information only (dates of employment, job title, reason for leaving etc.)
- checking doubtful information by telephone. (Write first to arrange this.)
- providing a structure or short questionnaire for the referee to follow.

6 The Follow-Up Process

Information about effectiveness of the recruitment and selection process is needed for three reasons:

- To seek improvements in policies and procedures
- To calculate costs; recruitment and selection is an expensive part of personnel management practice
- To provide feedback into human resource planning. For example it may be very difficult to fill

certain jobs. This will require information about the nature of the jobs and of the people required to perform them.

Follow-up is a difficult exercise. If a company recruits graduates and a large proportion leave within a year, where does the fault lie? In the recruitment and selection process? Or in the training programme? Or in the nature of the tasks they are required to perform? In the salaries paid? Or may the reason be demand for their skills elsewhere in the labour market? Evaluation will therefore need to be in depth.

Employee Follow-Up and Induction

Studies have shown that, where attention is given to their systematic introduction, the rate of labour turnover among new employees is lower. The existence of what has been termed the 'induction crisis' gives us a rationale for the development of techniques which aim generally to ease the entry of the individual into the organization.

Ways of Reducing the Effects of the Induction Crisis

- Obtain better information about candidates during recruitment and selection. This should improve selection decisions
- Give candidates better information about the job on offer. To some degree, people select themselves for jobs. This may include information which will cause candidates to withdraw or to refuse an offer of employment, should one be forthcoming. Some advertisements for social workers, for example, say: 'Want to be run off your feet, overworked, underappreciated? . . . Then join our busy team.' In this way, new recruits at least know what to expect.
- Improve the induction process. (This is covered later in this chapter.)

The Aims of the Induction Process

These are:

- To make the new employee efficient as quickly as possible
- To encourage the new employee to become committed to the organization and thus less likely to leave quickly
- To familiarize the new employee with the job so that the feeling of being 'out of place' is quickly dispelled.

7 The Induction Process

Those who have worked in organizations for some time forget what it felt like to be new. They take for granted their ways of working, the language they use at work and the accepted ways of dealing with colleagues, superiors, subordinates and clients. Departments, committee and other working groups are frequently referred to by initials.

Recently, I was involved in an organization with an 'IR' group. My own background led me to believe that this was an 'industrial relations group'. I was wrong! 'IR' in this case stood for 'information retrieval' – very confusing to the newcomer! Another example of the 'taken-for-granted' nature of organizational life comes from research I did in the hairdressing industry. A new apprentice in a high-class salon was asked by a stylist to buy some sandwiches for an important client from a neighbouring snack bar. She returned with them in a paper bag and gave them to the client not realizing that this was unacceptable behaviour. Someone who 'knew the ropes' would have transferred the sandwiches to a plate before delivering them! Her embarrassment at this and other incidents led her to seek other employment.

From such stories, you should recognize the importance of giving attention to the induction process. New employees usually want to do a 'fair day's work for a fair day's pay'. They want to be accepted by their colleagues and to feel generally comfortable in the organization and in their job. Management wants workers who will quickly become efficient and committed. The aim of the induction process is to meet the needs of both parties in a mutually acceptable way.

Induction programmes must be designed to fit the particular characteristics of the job and of its organizational context.

On the first day, it is important to ensure that new employees:

- do not feel lost or foolish
- do not endanger themselves or other people because they are not given vital safety information.

Provided this is done, there are no other hard and fast rules about this stage of the induction process. It is generally unwise to communicate a great deal of information orally to new employees at this time. The stress of the first day in a new environment can be a 'culture shock'. The danger is that little will be remembered. It is wise to provide written 'back-up' to vital information communicated orally for this reason. An employee handbook is useful here. Its contents should include:

- A brief description of the organization – numbers employed, locations, products, etc.
- The basic conditions of employment – pay scales, holidays, pension arrangements, hours of work
- Sickness arrangements – notification, pay, certification
- Disciplinary and grievance procedures
- Trade union membership and collective bargaining arrangements
- Staff purchase arrangements and other 'perks'

- Travelling and subsistence arrangements
- Medical and welfare facilities
- Canteen facilities
- Health and safety arrangements
- Education and training policies and facilities.

This list is by no means exhaustive. The content of employee handbooks varies depending on such organizational characteristics as numbers employed, jobs performed, managerial policies and practices. Handbooks need not be glossy and should be written clearly and concisely with the information needs of the employee as the focus.

Induction Training

Many organizations run induction courses as a formal mechanism for the induction of new employees. If it is decided that an induction course might be beneficial to some or all new employees, careful attention must be given to content and timing. The needs of new entrants differ considerably. For example, new members of management probably require more detailed information about organization structure, policies and practices than will more junior clerical staff or manual workers. There are probably disadvantages in arranging for new employees to attend off-the-job induction courses too early. Initially, it is likely that they will be keen to familiarize themselves with the immediate requirements of the job which they are to perform. However, in a reatively short time they should be ready to know more about the organization in which they work.

Departmental Induction

A more informal induction process is probably just as important as a training course. For the new employee it may be far more important, at least in the initial stages of employment with an organization, to get to know one's colleagues and the nature of one's job, than to be given more general information about the employing organization.

In a large organization, it is likely that the personnel or training department will carry responsibility for the formal part of the induction process, but line managers and supervisors should not abdicate responsibility for the less formal process. New employees at least should be welcomed by their departmental manager even if – as commonly occurs – the immediate supervisor is mainly responsible for introducing the new employee to the job and to workmates. In small companies, where it would not be economic to organize a formal induction course, it is even more vital that someone (probably the supervisor) is responsible for introducing each new employee to the organization. A checklist of items to be covered would be a useful aid to ensure this is carried out effectively.

A Final Word

Throughout this section we have stressed the need to design induction procedures with the perspective and needs of the new employee in mind. To ensure that this has been achieved, it will be useful to review systematically the experiences of newcomers and other relevant employees (for example, supervisors, training and personnel specialists) so that unsatisfactory elements can be changed. Many organizations do not do this; there is a plethora of film and video material about organizations which is either too remote from the newcomers' likely experience or so facile that it leads only to mockery. New employees might be prepared to voice such criticisms if only they were asked to speak.

3 The Law and the Rights of the New Employee

1 The Legal Framework of Employers' Rights

Employment law contains provisions relating both to collective bargaining, or the rights of employees as trade unionists, and to the rights at work of individual employees. This book is concerned mainly with the latter area. The collective rights of employees in law are dealt with in *Industrial Relations* by Chris Brewster, (Pan Management Guides).

Employees' legal rights are created not only by Acts of Parliament. They derive also from case law. The English legal system can be distinguished from that of most other countries by the extent to which judges and tribunals must follow the decisions of higher courts unless they feel that the facts of the previous cases were substantially different. In this way they are said to be bound by 'judicial precedent'.

It is normally sufficient for managers to be aware of the main statutory provisions of employment law. This book aims to make you aware of these. However, you should be clear about the limits of your knowledge if you are called on to make decisions which might affect employees' legal rights. Specialist help is available from a range of sources – the Advisory, Conciliation and Arbitration Service (ACAS), employers' associations, private consultants and personnel or legal departments in larger organizations.

The Role of ACAS in Individual Rights Legislation

ACAS automatically receives copies of all individual claims to tribunals except those which are concerned only with redundancy compensation. Normally employees must make claims within three months of the event which forms the basis of their complaint. ACAS has specialist conciliation officers to assist in these cases. Often this official contacts the parties or their representatives and tries to help them reach a settlement before the case goes to a tribunal. About half the cases raised by employees result in a settlement at this stage.

Industrial Tribunals

If conciliation fails, the case will go to a tribunal. Tribunals, which are organized on a regional basis, consist of a legally qualified chairman and two 'side members', representing the two sides of industry. These are selected from a panel drawn up by the Secretary of State for Employment from nominations from the Confederation of British Industry, the Department of Employment, the Trades Union Congress and other bodies. In practice, nominees often have trade union, personnel management or other relevant work experience.

Tribunal procedure is relatively informal. Employees are often represented by trade union officials and employers sometimes use legal representatives. Tribunal decisions do not set precedent but they are bound by the decisions of higher courts. They do not normally award costs in favour of the winning party, though they may do so where one party has acted 'frivolously or vexatiously'.

Appeals Against Tribunal Decisions

If there is an appeal on a point of law against a tribunal's decision, the case will go to the Employment Appeal Tribunal (EAT), thence to the Court of Appeal and ultimately to the House of Lords. These latter courts are part of the mainstream of the English legal system. However, the EAT deals specifically with appeals from industrial tribunals. As compared with other courts of law, its procedures are relatively informal but it has all the powers of the High Court. Each case is heard by a judge and normally two lay members, drawn from a panel with specialist knowledge of industrial relations.

Here is a flowchart which summarizes the progress of an individual claim against an employer under one of the statutes which comprise employment legislation.

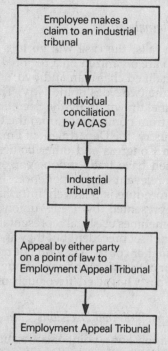

Figure 3. The progress of an employment law case from inception to a hearing by the Employment Appeal Tribunal

2 The Law and the Rights of Job Applicants

Job applicants are protected from discrimination by employers on grounds of:

- sex
- race
- marital status
- colour
- nationality
- ethnic or national origin.

The main statutes here are the Sex Discrimination Act 1975 and the Race Relations Act 1976. Employers should also be aware of the Codes of Practice on Sex and Marriage Discrimination and Race Discrimination issued by the Equal Opportunities Commission and the Commission for Racial Equality respectively. These are not legally binding but are admissible as evidence of bad management practice before an industrial tribunal or court.

Other groups of job applicants protected by law to some degree are the disabled and those who have been convicted of offences. The relevant statutes here are the Disabled Persons (Employment) Acts 1944 and 1958, the Companies (Directors Report), (Employment of Disabled Persons) Regulations 1980 and the Rehabilitation of Offenders Act 1974.

What Is Discrimination?

Both the Race Relations Act and the Sex Discrimination Act define three kinds of discrimination.

Direct discrimination. This is easy to discern. For example, if all applicants for clerical work are required to be male or of a particular race, this clearly would constitute direct discrimination.

Indirect discrimination. This is more subtle and less easy to prove. A requirement that all prospective hospital porters must be able to pass an English language test and lift very heavy weights might be indirect discrimination. This would be the case if:

- the proportion of people of a particular racial group or sex who could comply with these conditions was demonstrably smaller than the proportion of people outside these groups

and

- the hospital management could not justify the conditions by showing that they were necessary and not merely convenient.

Previous cases have shown that employers cannot automatically justify on health and safety grounds the non-selection of applicants who speak poor English. Of course, staff must be able to understand safety notices, but the testing of proficiency in English is not the only way to ensure that the requirements of the Health and Safety at Work Act are met. One way is to translate safety notices and other information into relevant languages. For illiterate employees it might be possible to use clearly understood symbols. Another alternative would be to provide safety training in the relevant language or to offer English language training.

Whether requiring job applicants to lift heavy weights is potentially discriminatory against women depends on whether it could be proved that fewer women than men could meet the strength test laid down by the hospital. If this was the case, management would have to demonstrate that a porter's job required employees to be able to lift the weights specified.

Victimization. The third type of illegal discrimination is where someone, who has brought proceedings, given evidence or made allegations in good faith against an employer, is treated less favourably than other people.

3 Coverage of the Anti-Discrimination Legislation

The sex and race discrimination legislation covers all aspects of employment. In this chapter we examine only its relevance to recruitment and selection.

Recruitment

Employers must not unlawfully discriminate against potential employees in any of the following ways:

- In the general arrangements for filling a vacancy; for example, a supervisor should not tell a personnel officer to recruit 'a man to replace Charlie'.
- In deciding who to appoint to fill a vacancy; for example, rejecting or omitting to consider applications from members of ethnic minorities.
- In offering different terms and conditions of employmen depending on the race or sex of the applicant.

There should be nothing in the wording of advertisements to suggest that jobs are open to some groups and not to others.

Selection

The method of filling vacancies can be discriminatory. There is evidence that word of mouth is more often used than formerly. This is likely to perpetuate the status quo of the organization's population structure in that white males are likely to introduce other white males to fill jobs. An investigation by the Commission for Racial

Equality into a London firm of bakers and confectioners concluded that this was a form of indirect discrimination. Since many potential employees approach organizations by telephoning or calling 'on spec', it is important that personnel department secretaries, receptionists and other 'gatekeepers' understand their responsibilities in law.

Interviews are likely places for discriminatory behaviour. There may be a tendency to attempt to replace a previous job incumbent with someone of similar outward characteristics. As a result interviewers may try to prove that outwardly dissimilar applicants could not cope with the demands of a job. For example, women who apply to be a member of a previously all male team of trainers may be asked how they would feel if they became a member of such a group and had to deal with mainly male course members. It is unlikely that male applicants would be asked these questions.

Genuine Occupational Qualifications (GOQ)

It is lawful to select workers of a particular sex or race when being a man or a woman or a member of a particular racial group is a genuine occupational qualification for the job. For example, a GOQ on grounds of sex would be lack of separate sleeping accommodation or toilets, where the job requires employees to 'live in' and it would be unreasonable to ask the employer to provide alternative accommodation for a worker of the opposite sex. Other examples of GOQs are:

- A female matron in an all girls' school
- a male lavatory attendant in a men's toilet
- A Chinese waiter in a Chinese restaurant

It is up to management to justify the existence of a GOQ if it is challenged by someone who feels unreasonably excluded from the job as a result.

Other Groups Protected from Discriminatory Recruitment Decisions

Apart from the race and sex discrimination legislation, there are only two other areas of statutory restriction on an employer's right to select employees.

Disabled workers. Employers with more than twenty regular workers must ensure that they employ a quota of registered disabled workers (usually three per cent) unless an exempting permit has been issued to them. In addition, certain jobs, for example car park attendant, must not be filled by an able-bodied person unless no disabled person is available. Companies employing more than 250 staff must ensure that directors' reports contain a statement describing policy on the employment of the disabled, including that on recruitment.

Those convicted of offences. Individuals are allowed to 'wipe out' some offences after a specified period. Depending upon the sentence imposed, a conviction for an offence is said to be 'spent' between six months and ten years after the offence was committed, provided that no further serious offence was committed during the rehabilitation period. Applicants in this position need not normally disclose their spent convictions when applying for a job. This is not the case for doctors, dentists, health or social workers, accountants, lawyers and others whose work involves direct responsibility for human or financial resources.

4 The Contract of Employment

Once the employer makes an offer of employment to an individual and this is accepted, a contract of employment comes into existence. This need not take the form of a written contract, though it is customary for it to do so. The details of the contract are known as its terms and conditions. A contract of employment can be seen as an exchange of work for wages. For it to be a legal exchange, neither party should feel that they made the contract under duress and each should be free to enter into it. A contract of employment would lack legality, for example, if a boss threatened physically to harm a prospective employee who refused an offer of employment. Also, if either side misrepresented themselves prior to the contract being agreed, the contract would be invalid. For example, if an applicant claimed to have a qualification specified for entry to a job and subsequently this proved not to be so, a dismissal would be legal.

An employer must give each employee a written statement of the main particulars of employment within thirteen weeks of the date of engagement. This should include:

- Employer's name
- Date employment began
- Job title
- Rate of pay (including overtime rates and annual increments)
- Hours of work
- Holiday entitlement
- Sick pay and procedures
- Pension rights
- Amounts of notice
- Disciplinary and grievance procedure.

In some cases, items need not be specified in detail so long as there is clear reference to a place where the relevant documents can be found. Employees also must have reasonable access to such information. In this case, employers need not notify employees individually of all changes in their terms and conditions of employment. For example, reference may be made to collective agreements with trade unions. In this case, management should ensure that employees are aware that changes in terms and conditions of employment will be i. porated into written agreements with trade unions. i. is legitimate whether or not all employees are membe of a union recognized for collective bargaining purposes.

The Significance of the Written Statement

The written statement is not a contract of employment. As stated above, the contract need not be in writing. However, employees who do not receive written particulars of their employment within thirteen weeks of the date of engagement, or who receive particulars which they believe to be incorrect, can take the matter to an industrial tribunal for an order that the employer supplies such a statement.

Not all workers must have written particulars by law. The major exclusions are:

- Registered dock workers
- Husbands and wives of the employer
- Crown and some National Health Service employees
- Employees who work wholly or mainly outside the UK
- Employees whose written particulars have already been embodied in a written contract, for example as required in apprenticeship contracts.

Express and Implied Terms of a Contract of Employment

All contracts of employment contain 'express terms'; that is those conditions which are expressed verbally or in writing. 'Implied' terms are assumed to form part of every contract of employment under the common law. These are general obligations to be followed by employers and employees.

eral Obligations

nplied duties can be summarised as:

- nd willing to work
- onable orders
- use reasonable care and skill
- To be trustworthy.

Employers' General Obligations

These include the duty:

- to pay agreed wages
- not to make deductions from pay without the employee's consent
- to provide work (in some cases)
- to provide a safe system of work
- to obey the law.

4   Employee Involvement

Whether or not employees live up to the expectations of those who selected them depends on management's success in motivating them to work effectively. In other words:

1   Capability × Motivation = Performance

Though this equation is oversimplified, it stresses the crucial importance of motivation to the employment relationship.

Do Employees Work for Love or Money?

The research evidence is contradictory. Some research subjects stress the importance of pay. By contrast, the majority of workers seem convinced they would continue to work if they inherited a fortune or won the football pools. There is anecdotal evidence to support this from workers who have found themselves lucky enough to be able to make this choice. Clearly, for them, money is not the only source of motivation.

A further complication is that motivation to work is affected by:

- The nature of the job
- Age
- Experience of life and work
- Plans for the future.

Also, feelings about work may change from time t

time. For example, while doing the job workers may be concerned only that it is challenging and interesting and gives opportunities to be creative. When the union which represents them is negotiating the next pay increase, however, they may be more concerned about the money they are paid.

Many managers have their own 'pet' theories about ways of encouraging employees to work harder. If it is believed that workers are most likely to perform effectively if their work is interesting, job design techniques may be used to try to increase productivity. The belief that an attractive working environment is vital to workers' motivation, will result probably in expenditure of time and effort on the selection of attractive potted plants and the design of colour schemes.

Most managements have traditionally operated on a 'carrot and stick' theory of motivation, believing that provision of appropriate incentives, particularly money, encourages workers to expend the maximum effort. This is the theory behind many payment systems. Not surprisingly, workers have materialistic values; those who perform dull jobs may have little other than money by which to be motivated!

Maslow's Hierarchy of Needs

This is the most famous classification of human needs based on the assumption that people have wants directed to specific goals. Maslow postulated five main categories of need arranged in a HIERARCHY – i.e. once a lower order need is satisfied, the individual becomes motivated by needs which exist at the next highest level of the hierarchy.

In figure 4, we see that Maslow assumed that, if people have enough to eat and drink, their attention turns to the need for security – for example, the worker's concern to avoid redundancy. Once this is satisfied, attention turns to relationships with other people – the need to feel wanted and loved. At this stage workers are concerned with their membership of a work group and of an organization. The higher-order needs for self-esteem or status and recognition in the eyes of the world, and, finally, for self-actualization or the achievement of full potential, become motivators only when the lower order needs have been satisfied.

Figure 4. Maslow's hierarchy of needs

A problem with this needs hierarchy theory is that many workers do not cease to be concerned about money once their basic needs have been met. We can all think of wealthy people whose behaviour demonstrates that they are far from satisfied.

Employees also seem to be motivated by different aspects of the job in different situations. Thus, on the same day, they may demand more money in a negotiating meeting and more satisfying work on the job. It seems that two or more levels of the hierarchy may be operating at the same time.

Despite these drawbacks, Maslow's hierarchy has value for managers and personnel specialists, suggesting that:

- the nature of the motivation to work is complex
- there is no single overriding source of motivation
- managers cannot afford to rest on their laurels, after awarding workers a generous pay increase, for example. Demands at a higher level of the hierarchy should be anticipated.

Herzberg's 'Two Factor' Theory of Motivation

In the view of this American organizational psychologist, employees' wants can be divided into SATISFIERS, or motivators, and DISSATISFIERS, or hygiene factors. The first group are effective motivators because they are a source of personal growth. They include:

- Achievement
- Recognition
- Advancement
- Responsibility
- The work itself.

By contrast, the presence of 'hygiene' factors prevents dissatisfaction and poor performance. Such elements of job content must be present if the employee is to feel fairly treated. Hygiene factors include:

- Wages or salaries
- Supervision
- Working conditions
- Company policy and administration.

Like Maslow's need hierarchy, this theory has been criticized on grounds of oversimplification. Nevertheless, it carries the vital message that, no matter how important the job is, if the work itself is dull and meaningless, the employee will be apathetic.

Orientation To Work

Sociologists analyse the degree to which wider social forces impinge on work behaviour. They need to know what employees expect from and value in their work. The term 'orientation to work' is used to categorise employees' preferences about various aspects of work and its rewards. In J. H. Goldthorpe et al., *The Affluent Worker: Industrial Attitudes and Behaviour* (Cambridge 1948), Goldthorpe identifies the prevalence of an 'instrumental' orientation among highly paid manual workers. These people tended to see work as a means to an end, a way of earning a living to support an affluent lifestyle. For them, work was not a central life interest; work involvement was calculative.

There are other work orientations. For example, some employees have a bureaucratic attachment to their employing organization. These are mainly white-collar workers who have some expectation of upward movement in the organization. For them, career development is important; work is a central life interest. Involvement in work is moral rather than simply calculative. Some employees are 'cosmopolitans', seeing themselves not as members of a particular organization but as members of a professional or occupational group. The main group with which they identify lies outside the firm rather than inside it. For them, work too is a central life interest but their orientation is to opportunities in the labour market generally rather than within the organization in which they happen to be currently employed.

Direct Participation as a means of Encouraging Employee Commitment

Methods of direct employee participation include:

- job enrichment and other methods of work restructuring

- autonomous work groups
- quality circles
- suggestion schemes.

Restructuring Work to Encourage Efficiency and Commitment

There is now wide agreement that the highly specialized and routine jobs prevalent in much of industry, commerce and public service organizations:

- do not satisfy needs for personal growth and fulfilment
- can result in psychological strain and somatic complaints – stress is not restricted to those who occupy managerial roles
- do not use employees' full abilities
- are frustrating and may encourage unproductive acts ranging from shoddy work to literally throwing a spanner in the works
- can result in absenteeism , wildcat strikes and refusal to cooperate with management.

Efforts to promote more positive employee commitment have, thus far, affected only a small proportion of the labour force. Yet experiments in job redesign have demonstrated the opportunities for increased performance and satisfaction.

What are the Options in Redesigning Jobs?

The job of supermarket checkout operator is notorious for its incessant tedium. Here are three options for its redesign:

- The inclusion of one or more other tasks at the same level of difficulty within the operator's job; for example, both for packing the customer's shopping and for entering prices into the till. This is known as 'job enlargement'.

- Another option is 'job rotation', whereby all assistants are moved between various routine tasks such as shelf-filling, checkout operating and, where relevant, serving customers on specialist counters.
- A third option needs more radical redesign of the job to add elements involving responsibility. This probably would mean adding elements of the supervisor's job – signing cheques, exchanging faulty goods and dealing with customer complaints. It also might involve the work group in decisions about allocation of overtime. This is known as 'job enrichment'.

Examples of the first two options exist in many supermarkets since they do coincide with the 'don't do as you think do as you're told' style of management. They have been criticized as merely adding one 'Mickey Mouse job' to another. There is evidence that job enlargement and rotation can reduce fatigue or boredom provided that workers are happy with the changes involved. However, there is little evidence of increased productivity and the motivational effects of the changes seem to wear off once the new tasks become familiar. Some employees dislike job rotation because it breaks up established work groups.

Job Enrichment

By contrast job enrichment seems to create opportunities for increased performance and satisfaction. Generally, it has three elements:

- Reduced repetitiveness of work
- Incorporation of elements of related jobs into the enriched job – stock reordering, inspection and maintenance into manual jobs, for example
- Delegation of decision making – for manual jobs

this may involve personal responsibility for work scheduling and planning.

Trade unions argue that increases in responsibility must be financially rewarded; workers do not live by job satisfaction alone.

Other problems for management resulting from job enrichment can include the cost of investment in new technology and an initial fall in productivity as people adjust to new jobs.

Benefits claimed from work restructuring include reduced labour turnover and absenteeism, improvements in both quality and quantity of work and improvements in employee relations and job satisfaction.

Autonomous Work Groups

These are an extension of job enrichment in which a work group is given limited responsibility for immediate production planning and for task allocation. Most experiments in this form of employee involvement have taken place in Scandinavia. At Volvo, the car assembly line was scrapped to provide a more favourable environment for group working. However, while increases in organizational efficiency have been noted in these experiments, the degree to which management has relinquished control of production is limited. While workers have taken over some of the tasks of first-line supervisors, managers above this level have renounced few of their decision-making powers.

Quality Circles

These have been imported into the UK as part of an attempt to increase efficiency by 'learning from the Japanese'. Supervisors and work groups are provided with training in quality control and other problem-solving techniques. They are encouraged to attempt to identify and solve operating problems using specialists where necessary. The evidence suggests that quality circles can contribute to improvements in efficiency provided that all concerned are committed to the practices involved and management are willing to listen carefully and responsively to employee proposals. We can certainly identify similarities between Japan and the UK which account for the success of quality circles in some British companies:

- rising aspirations and increased education of workers
- the perceived need to reduce the specialized and routine nature of many production and clerical jobs
- the need to increase the commitment of many employees both to the employing organization and to the jobs they perform.

Nevertheless, there are many differences between employment relationships in Japan and in the UK which should prompt careful thought before any decision is taken to introduce quality circles.

Suggestion Schemes

These are some of the oldest forms of direct employee participation but only rarely have they been successful. A reason is that employees have tended not to be involved in the design or operation of these schemes; frequently, decisions about the acceptance or rejection of employee suggestions are made by a committee of managers with no obligation to give reasons for their decisions. The committee may take time to communicate its deliberations. Also, managers and supervisors often feel that suggestions made by those for whom they have responsibility are critical of their performance. Conflict can arise over the size of the monetary or other reward for the submission of a successful suggestion. Evidence suggests that the criteria for the introduction of a successful scheme are:

- commitment of all levels of management
- involvement and support of recognized trade unions
- involvement of employees during the evaluation of their suggestions
- clear recognition that the emergence of suggestions is not a criticism of those occupying managerial, supervisory or specialist roles
- efficient administration of the scheme.

2 Employee Participation in Managerial Decision Making

In this section, we examine ways in which employees can become involved in managerial decision making through representatives. Such indirect participation can be expressed diagramatically, see figure 5.

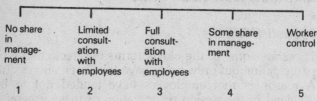

No share in management	Limited consultation with employees	Full consultation with employees	Some share in management	Worker control
1	2	3	4	5

Figure 5. Scale of employee involvement in managerial decision making

No Share in Managerial Control

Here the managerial prerogative is absolute. Employees have no share in managerial decision making.

Limited Consultation

The UK has a tradition of joint consultation in which management has consulted rather than negotiated with employees through committees established for this purpose. Unions have been unhappy with this because of the tendency for management to give information after decisions have been taken. In addition, such committees often have had their scope limited to the discussion of 'tea and toilet rolls'. There has been an increase in the number of organizations with such committees over the last decade.

Full Consultation

This occurs through committees constituted in the same way as those described above, except that, here, employees or their representatives are given information on a very broad range of subjects by management. Production, marketing and financial plans as well as personnel matters are discussed. Yet, though mutually acceptable decisions are sought, employees are not able to control managerial decision making.

Though joint consultation has a bad reputation in some quarters because of the trivial nature of its subject matter, it can be a very useful communication mechanism if effectively organized and used.

Some Share in Management

Some managers are happy to involve employees up to the second or third stage of the scale in figure 5. Once this point is exceeded, many feel that their power to control the employment relationship is seriously affected. By contrast, union representatives tend to see consultation as a useful floor from which to achieve greater influence over managerial decision making. Collective bargaining has been the traditional way by which unions have achieved some influence over managerial decision making, but only in the limited area of terms and conditions of employment. More recently, there has been some attempt by unions to increase the scope of collective bargaining to include aspects of financial, market and production planning Agreements to negotiate the introduction of new technology have become more common. However, employee efforts to gain a greater say in managerial decision making in this way have been constrained by high levels of unemployment, with its consequent effect on trade union power. Hence, recently, there has been less immediate need for management to share power to contain challenges by employees.

Other schemes which give workers a share in management are those for the election of worker directors to the boards of organizations. These have been confined mainly to the nationalized industries, though there are a few less publicized schemes in the private sector. The existence of worker directors cannot change quickly the relationship between management and employees. However, those in favour of such schemes argue that, in the long run, they will lead to better relations between management and employees, since board level decision making will take account of the employee viewpoint. Despite such potential for improved industrial relations, many managers and trade unionists have reservations about worker director schemes. Though more pressure for these has come from the European Economic Community, at present there seems little likelihood that the UK will legislate for such a change.

Worker Control

Here, employees totally control the organization, often through a worker cooperative. They hire managers to implement their decisions. Profits are shared by the employees. Generally in the UK over recent years, worker cooperatives have been set up by employees anxious to protect their livelihoods when their employing organizations foundered. Many of them, such as the *Scottish Daily News*, Kirkby Manufacturing and Engineering and Triumph Motorcycles, subsequently failed. However, it would be unfair to conclude from these examples that such organizations are bound to fail. After all, they were sold to employees only because their owners had been unable to make them pay. In a few cases organizations have been given to employees out of idealism on the part of the owner. Scott Bader, a small chemicals manufacturer, is an example.

3 The Challenge for Management

Probably management is most straightforward when employees have no share in organization decision making. In these circumstances, the job of the manager is to tell employees what they are required to do and to ensure that they do it. All planning, control and decision making rests with management. When employees participate in the managerial process, managers need information and skills to cope with the consequent changes in organizational decision making. (See figure 6.)

Thus, decisions about employee involvement should not be taken without an analysis of the implications for managerial jobs together with an assessment as to whether managers can cope with subsequent changes in their roles. In general, such changes require managers to be more flexible. More detailed analysis of the new skill requirements is likely to show the need for:

■ improved communication skills
■ improved written and oral presentation skills

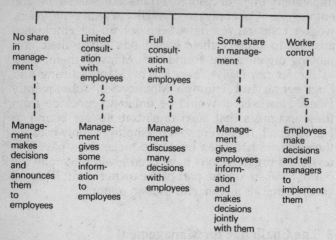

Figure 6. Implications of employee participation for managerial skills and style

- improved interpersonal and especially group work skills.

In addition, managers involved with employee representatives in indirect participation schemes will need skills analogous to those used in collective bargaining. However, the 'win-lose' tactics often used there are not appropriate. The skills involved are those of joint decision making.

5 Appraising Performance

'Getting the best out of people' is a crude term for management's key target in respect of employees. Performance appraisal rests on the assumption that, if employees' performance is scrutinized and feedback given, the motivation to work more effectively should increase.

1 What Is Performance Appraisal?

The dictionary definition of the verb 'appraise' is 'to fix a price for' or 'to value an object or thing'. In personnel management, 'performance appraisal' denotes concern with the process of valuing the employee's worth to the organization, with a view to increasing it.

What is the Purpose of Performance Appraisal?

Management's objectives in appraising employee performance are:

- To help improve current performance
- To assess training and development needs
- To assess future potential for promotion
- To give employees feedback on their performance
- To counsel employees on career opportunities

Who is Appraised?

Managerial, professional and technical staff, and those participating in training schemes, are more likely to be appraised than people in routine secretarial and clerical jobs. One reason is the association between appraisal and training and career development.

Designing an Appraisal System

Appraisal systems must suit the company culture. However, in designing appraisal systems, it is useful to examine recent developments. These show:

- increasing criticism of appraisal systems which attempt to measure personality characteristics such as loyalty, commitment or drive
- increased emphasis on more objective, job-related criteria and objectives – a 'results-oriented approach'
- more involvement of employees in their own appraisal
- more concentration on improving performance in the current job rather than assessing future potential.

We shall examine each in turn.

Personality based Appraisal Systems

It is difficult for managers to make valid judgements about subordinates on such qualities as intelligence, initiative or loyalty. Imagine a manager attempting to assess the intelligence of a subordinate for appraisal purposes.

- First, an understanding of the nature of intelligence is required
- Second, the manager must be competent to judge the degree to which it exists in other people
- Third, can it be assumed that all subordinates exhibit all their intelligence in their jobs?
- Fourth, all subordinates must be assessed in the

same way against the manager's definition of intelligence

■ Fifth, it probably will be necessary to give feedback to the employee on the results of the appraisal. It may be difficult to justify an assessment based on such a personality trait.

Research has shown that, whatever the chosen personality characteristic, appraisal tends to imply that women and members of other minority groups are less well equipped than their white male counterparts. In appraisal, as in selection, the roots of prejudice lie close to the surface. More objective ways of making judgements are vital.

Results Orientated Appraisal Systems or Performance Reviews

Fair judgements of performance must

■ be capable of more objective judgement by appraisers
■ be genuinely related to job performance.

Having thus justified an emphasis on job-related criteria of performance, the next step is to find the most appropriate measures of job performance.

Three general methods of deriving such performance measures are:

■ analysis of work content – documents, files etc.
■ questionnaires about job performance
■ analysis of key problems experienced by job holders.

Analysis of Work Content

In designing a performance review system for personnel specialists it would be useful to examine the documents they produce – interview reports, records of negotiations with trade unions and so on.

It would be necessary to establish the key skills in drawing up such documents. For the job of a personnel specialist this might include:

- clarity of expression
- conciseness
- methodical storage of information
- logical structure of reports.

However, by no means all the work of such specialists comprises written records. Much time is spent talking to other people in interviews and meetings, formal or informal. Therefore the content of such exchanges can also be analysed for key skills.

2 Questionnaires about Job Performance

Managers can be asked to complete questionnaires to describe the most and least effective performer in a particular job. Detailed statistical analysis of such questionnaires should give a profile of an effective job holder against which individuals' actual job performances can be measured.

Analysis of Key Problems Experienced by Job Holders

Employees can be asked to describe the most difficult problem they have experienced at work. This is often called the critical incident method. A large number of such incidents are analysed for trends, commonality and so on. These can be used to identify key skills.

Rating Performance Using Job-Related Measures

Key criteria of performance, thus established, became

yardsticks of effective performance against which managers are asked to rate subordinates. Often rating scales where employees are rated as excellent, very good, adequate, or below the required standard on each criteria of effective job performance are used. However, these definitions of performance are unhelpful. Managers' definitions of 'excellent', 'very good' and so on will differ. Only trained appraisers, using common yardsticks, should use such scales. In addition, employees labelled as 'below standard' may become disillusioned or decide to live up to their reputation. Improvement in employee performance is more likely to result from joint agreement between manager and subordinate about ways of achieving this.

Job-related Objectives

Many experienced practitioners argue that performance reviews are more effective motivators if they involve the setting of specific job-related objectives. Six or so key performance measures can be selected at the appraisal interview as relevant target areas for the employee for the next year. These can then be turned into specific objectives. For example, a key performance measure for a training specialist might be 'the design and implementation of management development programmes'. An objective for a particular trainer might be 'to investigate the detailed training needs of line managers in accountancy and finance, to design a short course (not more than five days' duration) and to run three such courses each for twelve line managers within the next six months.'

The advantages of such performance reviews are that they should be relevant to the personal needs of the employee and to the requirements for effective job performance. They encourage both appraiser and appraised to look carefully at what actually has been achieved in the immediate past as well as what may realistically be expected over the year ahead.

Employee Involvement in Appraisal

Appraisal systems are now more 'open' than formerly. There is more likelihood that employees will be shown either all or part of their appraisal reports. This should increase employees' motivation to improve their job performance. Many managers find 'open' appraisal threatening because there is pressure on the appraiser to make the appraisal as complete and constructive as possible. Bland phrases and generalizations are likely to be challenged by employees together with the more obvious inaccuracies which indicate the managers' ignorance of the real nature of the employee's job. The trend towards more openness has been accompanied by greater emphasis on results-oriented approaches. It is easier to justify assessment of performance based on the key results areas of the job rather than on more nebulous, and less obviously relevant, personality traits.

Current Performance v. Future Potential

Many managers do not see assessment of potential as a prime purpose of appraisal. Many companies now encourage people to make sideways moves to increase experience, knowledge and skills before, or instead of, upward progression. As a result performance appraisal is concerned more with current performance than with future potential.

Potential Reviews

Separate systematic reviews of potential are useful for those for whom career or management development is contemplated. Many managers find the assessment of potential difficult since their experience of the individual is limited to observations of performance in the current job. For this reason a 'grandfather' figure – more senior manager – is often used to avoid some of the prejudices of the immediate manager. Another way of assessing potential is to use an assessment centre (see Chapter 8).

Who Will Appraise?

Appraisal is commonly undertaken by the immediate supervisor. Sometimes, as mentioned in the previous section, a more senior manager is used in an overseeing role. More open appraisal implies a shift in the control of appraisal from the appraiser to the appraisee. Some companies use self-appraisal schemes where the employee takes the lead. This may be useful where employees' work is frequently unsupervised and elements of it are not easily assessable – for example, professional employees. In similar circumstances, peer group appraisal can be used, where each employee nominates one or two colleagues, to undertake appraisal. However, in most organizations managers prefer to retain control of appraisal.

Appraisal – a Ritual of Employment?

Views on the value of appraisal differ widely. Whether an appraisal system will be helpful to the employment relationship depends on the nature of the organization, the appraisal system and the skills of those employed. The general advantages and disadvantages are summarized below.

Advantages

■ In an appraisal interview boss and subordinate

have a formal opportunity for a candid exchange of views, provided that the relationship between them and the nature of the appraisal scheme encourage this

- Good performance appraisal systems encourage line managers to think systematically about career and management development for their subordinates having reviewed the detailed nature of the work currently being undertaken
- Performance appraisal can provide very useful data for the analysis of training needs and the design of training programmes.

Disadvantages

- The relationship between boss and subordinate is frequently fragile. It can be harmed by the necessity for the manager to formalize and articulate feelings about subordinates
- Even after training, some managers have difficulty with appraisal interviews
- Many appraisal systems involve too much paperwork. This hinders rather than helps.

Conditions Necessary for Successful Appraisal Schemes

Despite all the criticism the evidence is that the popularity of appraisal has not declined. Over seventy per cent of organizations have appraisal systems and most of those who do not are small companies, where the process probably tends to occur informally.

So are there any general lessons to be learnt before introducing an appraisal system? Careful analysis of the organization's particular circumstances is vital before embarking on this difficult path. Here are some suggestions:

- Get top management support

- Plan and prepare carefully
- Beware glossy consultancy packages or other companies' schemes
- Give oral introductory presentations to managers, trade union representatives and employees
- Prepare explanatory pamphlets for all those involved
- Train appraisers
- Make sure that the scheme is effectively implemented
- Ensure that promises made in appraisal interviews; for example for further training, are carried out
- Avoid close linkage with pay
- Closely monitor the operation of the scheme.

Lastly, keep it simple! If a vast bureaucracy can be avoided do so. Some companies have found that the key to successful appraisal lies in the appraisal interview. Little need be written down or recorded centrally, for example, by the personnel department other than agreed key result areas and training needs.

6 Training for Current Jobs

What is training? From childhood we learn to cope with living. Is this training or is it education? These terms are often used as if they were synonymous. They are not and an understanding of the differences between them is important to understanding the training process in business organizations. Both are processes which help people learn but they differ in orientation and objectives. It is probably simplest to define training as oriented towards the needs of the organization while education is oriented to the needs of the individual. These differences are summarized in figure 7.

1 Objectives of Training

The objectives of the training process in a work organization can be summarized as follows:

- To assist workers to perform at the optimum level in current jobs
- To develop employees for future jobs

Training Policy

To supply the organization with effective manpower, the training function must be acquainted with, or involved in, the corporate planning process. Training policies must be related to, and supportive of, corporate policies.

To take an example, Fred's Food Processing Company, a manufacturer of frozen foods, plans to acquire a

Characteristics of the learning process	Education	Training
Objectives	More abstract objectives geared to the needs of the individual and to society generally	Specific behaviourial objectives to make workers more effective in their jobs
Timescale	Generally a long-term process	Can be very short-term especially when concerned with the acquisition of specific skills
Content	Widely drawn content	Often fairly narrow content specific to the employee's work situation

Figure 7. Differences between education and training

chain of frozen food shops over the next two years. The company's training function needs to be involved in the implementation of this decision, so that, when the retail business is acquired, there is a trained labour force to run it. Fred intends to recruit an entirely new workforce for the retail operation. Here is Fred's training policy.

Fred's Food Processing Company
Statement of training policy

The aim of this policy is to ensure that all employees are assisted to develop themselves in order that they may make the best possible contribution to the achievement of company objectives.

In the training area it is our policy to:

1 Draw up a training plan with reference to company objectives.
2 Involve managers in the identification of training objectives for their units.
3 Base training on a thorough analysis of needs.
4 Provide employees with potential with opportunities for further training and development.
5 Have a specialist training department charged with responsibility for the development and implementation of training employees.
6 Provide induction training for all employees.
7 Provide day release for first qualification training for all staff between the ages of 16 and 25.
8 Provide training courses and other training facilities to satisfy needs identified by managers or specialist training staff.
9 All training will be funded from the training budget and must be authorized by the head of the training department.

Item 4 does not fit in with Fred's intention to recruit workers for the shops from the open market. Actions in breach of declared policy are likely to be very damaging to employee morale. Fred should advertise new posts within the manufacturing company before attempting to recruit new employees, unless he wishes to change this aspect of company policy.

2 A Systematic Approach to Training

Training can contribute to the effective use of the organization's resources, but only if approached systematically.

The phases of the training process are shown in figure 8. (The figure includes the links between training and company policy to emphasize the necessity for this integration.)

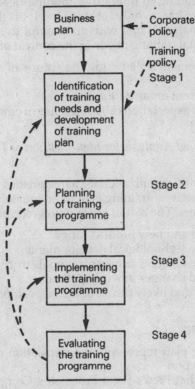

Figure 8. Training process

3 Stage One: The Identification of Training Needs

A training need can be defined as the gap between the requirements for skills and knowledge inherent in the job

and those possessed by the current job holder. It is vital
that this gap is adequately analysed to establish exactly
what training is required. (See figure 9.)

It is misleading to imply that training needs analysis
should take place only at the level of the job. A
thorough analysis starts with an attempt to assess total
organizational training needs in the context of:

■ management's plans for the future of the organization
■ the current organization structure
■ current expectations about the use of employees.

Organizational Analysis for Identification of Training Needs

An analysis of organizational characteristics and problems is necessary if training is to be adequately linked to
business plans. The sort of information required is:

■ existing and new product range
■ planned technological developments
■ planned changes to organizational structure
■ planned changes in work methods
■ current and likely future financial position.

Training Plans

The training plan represents the translation of training
needs into action.

Suppose that Fred's Food Processing Company loses
a number of unfair dismissal cases. Investigation of the
facts behind these dismissals reveals that one of the
problems was the inadequate handling of problem
employees by supervisors which was compounded by
their lack of understanding of employees' legal rights in
this area. An entry in the company training plan to
cover this might read:

TRAINING NEED	ESTIMATED BENEFIT	ACTION	RESPONSI-BILITY	TIME SCALE	BUDGET
handling of disciplinary cases by first-line supervisors	fewer industrial tribunal cases and the company will be more likely to win those which arise	plan and run two day training course for all first-line supervisors	training department	complete within six months	£2000

The process of training needs analysis at organizational level is summarized in figure 9.

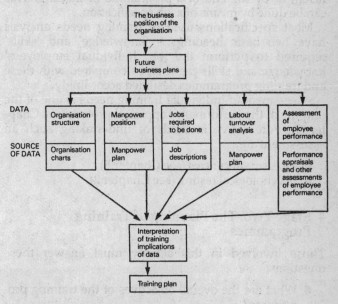

Figure 9. Training needs at organizational level

Training Needs Analysis at Individual Level

Before training programmes can be organized for individual employees, it is necessary to analyse their jobs for training purposes.

Job Analysis

In Chapter 2 we examined briefly the process of job analysis in recruitment and selection. However, the emphasis here is on those aspects of the job which make it difficult to learn. It is important to specify what procedures, techniques and skills the trainee must be proficient at by the end of a programme of training. This can be done by means of a job specification.

Most specifications used in training needs analysis have two basic headings – 'knowledge' and 'skills' required to perform the job. Individual employees' knowledge and skills can then be compared with these and training programmes designed accordingly.

Assessment of individual training needs is one of the outputs of the performance appraisal process (see Chapter 5). Alternative methods of undertaking such an assessment are:

- assessment centres (see Chapter 5)
- psychological testing (see Chapter 2).

4 Stage Two: The Planning of Training Programmes

Those involved in this activity must answer these questions:

- What are the overall objectives of the training programme?
- Where and when should training take place?
- What should be the content of the training programme?

- What learning methods should be used?

They also need to know who will undertake the training and who will adminster it.

Specification of Training Objectives

Ideally, the objective of a training programme should be expressed in terms of the behaviour expected of the trainee when training is complete. Thus, by the end of the programme outlined in the training plan extract on p.79, Fred's supervisors should be able to:

- demonstrate a working knowledge of the law on dismissal
- demonstrate improved skills in the handling of disciplinary interviews.

The objectives of training programmes should fit trainees' needs. Note that the first objective here is related to supervisors' needs for knowledge and their needs for improved skills.

Timing of Training Programmes

The main considerations are:

- the need to minimize disruption to the trainee's work group
- the trainee's view of the most appropriate time for training
- the optimum integration between job demands and the content of the training programme – it is not much use to send trainees on courses when there will not be any immediate opportunity to use newly acquired skills or knowledge
- the availability of trainers, training rooms and other necessary resources
- the need to work within budgetary contraints.

4 Location of Training Programmes

Off-the-Job at the Workplace

Most large organizations have a training centre or training room. The advantage of such 'in-house' provision is that it can encourage identification with the organization and thus the integration between work and training. Also, if all trainees are fellow employees, cross-fertilization of ideas and the breaking down of department barriers can occur. Possible disadvantages include the exertion of pressure on trainees to return to their jobs if a crisis arises, thus hampering learning.

On-the-Job Training at the Workplace

'Sitting by Nellie' has long been favoured as a means of passing job knowledge and skills to new employees. Learning can be put into practice straight away. However, the success of this approach depends very much on the quality of 'Nellie'. For best results management should:

- Ensure that 'Nellie' performs the job exactly in line with management's requirements
- Train 'Nellie' to be an effective teacher and coach (see Chapter 7, p.96.)

This will not overcome problems of work environment. The hustle and bustle of a busy office may not be conducive to training a typist to be an effective word processor operator.

External Courses

Sometimes it is not economic to design 'in-house' programmes to meet trainees' needs. In addition, development for managers and specialist staff, especially those which lead to formal qualifications, frequently have an educational orientation. Such provision is normally only available externally. The advantages of external courses are:

- the tuition may be better than within the organization
- trainees may feel freer to question and experiment
- mixing with people from other organizations may facilitate learning. For example, managers may learn that there are other options in the resolution of industrial relations problems by contact with their counterparts in other institutions.

5 The Use of Trainers

External trainers or consultants can be used to run training programmes or the organization can use suitable employees, usually training specialists. The relevant considerations here are:

- whether the training department or others available as trainers in the organization have sufficient expertise and time available to undertake the training programme
- what financial resources are available
- whether it is desirable to encourage trainees to learn about the relevant policies and practices of other organizations; external trainers are often able to help here.

When external trainers or consultants are used, it is vital to brief them properly with relevant details of the organization, the training needs analysis on which the programme is to be based, the backgrounds and expectations of the trainees and the training traditions of the organization.

Administration of Training

Good training administrators ensure that:

- clear joining instructions are sent to participants well before the start of the programme
- trainees understand the objectives of the programme
- training is uninterrupted and necessary services (training materials, meals, etc.) are available.

Content of Training Programme

The basis of our understanding of this subject lies in an area of psychology known as learning theory. Unfortunately, while the learning theorists have provided us with some pointers to the conditions under which training best takes place, they have been unable to find a solution for every case where training is necessary. Different people learn in different ways. Here is some guidance from learning theory which is relevant to the design of training programmes:

- Elements of new knowledge required by trainees must be identified and presented in a way which aids learning
- Learning is assisted if it can be related to the trainee's previous experience. Trainers should be familiar with the background of the trainees and should try to 'speak their language'
- Learning often occurs through experience. Trainees should be given the opportunity to use previous experience and to practise newly acquired skills and knowledge
- 'Learning how to learn' is a skill which trainees should be helped to acquire. Thus trainers should be prepared to provide access to asssistance with literacy and numeracy as well as generally to facilitate the learning process

- Trainees' rates and methods of learning very greatly. Older people, for example, differ from younger people in this respect
- Some trainees reach a standstill or plateau in their learning from time to time. Trainers must try to understand the reasons for this to help trainees to make further progress
- One of the most important influences on trainees' progress is their level of motivation. Trainers should be aware of factors likely to affect trainees' motivation.

Training Methods

These include:

- lectures
- one-to-one instruction
- conferences
- workshops
- case studies
- roleplay
- discussions
- experiential learning
- sensitivity training
- action learning
- brainstorming
- coaching
- projects
- distance learning or self-study.

These categories are not mutually exclusive. For example, experiential learning workshops can be run.

We lack space here to examine the relative merits of each method; however trainers must select methods which are suitable to the needs of trainees and to the resources available. It is very useful for this to be done in conjunction with the trainees after making sure they understand the aims and objectives of training. 'Variety is the spice of life' in training and a number of methods can usefully be combined. For example, trainers are frequently subject to pressure from line managers to shorten training programmes in the interests of short-term productivity. Trainers can accommodate such pressures sometimes by encouraging trainees to use well designed self-study texts. Attendance on a training programme can be used for learning in areas where participative methods must be used. However, self-study or distance learning is not without its problems for trainees. Some of these are:

- The link between the content of such materials and trainees' previous experience may not be readily apparent
- Trainees may reach learning plateau and find it difficult to progress
- Trainees may lack the study skills to cope with the material.

These potential disadvantages may be overcome wholly or in part if the trainee has a coach or mentor in the organization who is capable of assisting with learning problems. This may be a trainer or a trained manager.

6 Stage Three: Implementing Training Programmes

Selection of Appropriate Trainees for Training

Some points to bear in mind here are:

- SIZE OF THE GROUP. Participative methods such as roleplay cannot be conducted effectively with large numbers. Even with more teacher-centred methods, large numbers may be unhelpful; trainees can fail to become actively involved in their own learning
- MIX OF PARTICIPANTS. Work group members may be assisted to work together more effectively by a

common training experience such as a team-building workshop. Conversely individuals may develop ideas about possible new ways of solving work problems from a training programme which gives the opportunity to meet people from other departments or organizations

- THE PROCESS OF SELECTING TRAINEES SHOULD ALSO INVOLVE THEIR SUPERIORS. Much useful learning from training programmes fails to be carried back into the workplace. If the trainee's supervisor is responsible for pre-and-post-programme briefing, this is less likely to occur
- TRAINEES SHOULD WANT TO BE TRAINED. Only those employees who wish to undergo training should do so. Sometimes trainers have to work with course participants who have been told that they must be trained. In these cases there is resistance and little is achieved.

Give Trainees Feedback on Performance during the Training Programme

Informing trainees of their progress during training encourages appropriate behaviour to be continued and inappropriate behaviour to be dropped. It allows the trainer to discover whether trainees have learning problems and to help these to be overcome.

7 Stage Four: The Evaluation of Training Programmes

Evaluation Methods

Post-Programme Evaluation

Most trainers will tell you that the best time to get a positive reaction to a training programme from trainees is at the end of the last day. This action may not be valid in that the trainee is often in a state of euphoria at this time having been bombarded with ideas. It may be appropriate to administer a questionnaire at the end of the course which is clearly linked with the training which has been undertaken. It can be linked to a pre-course questionnaire to check the degree to which the course has come up to the trainee's expectations and has increased knowledge.

Because of the problems of administering such questionnaires at the end of the course, some trainers send them to participants weeks or months afterwards. This too has its disadvantages in that the response rate tends to be low. Also to be effective, evaluation must measure whether training objectives have been achieved; that is, whether the trainee's performance has been improved. Asking for trainees' reactions to a course or even attempting to measure improvements in their knowledge does not assess whether they are more effective employees as a result.

Other Training Evaluation Methods

Training is rarely evaluated with reference to:

- the behaviour of the individual employee on the job
- organizational performance in areas where training has been undertaken
- the degree to which the whole organization has benefited from training and development.

What is certain is that the further away you get from trainees' reactions to training the more difficult evaluation becomes. This is because other factors may be responsible for the changes detected. For example, suppose that the year after Fred's Food Processing Company sends all its supervisors on the training programme (outlined in the extract from the training on p.79), claims of unfair dismissal fall by fifty per cent and the company wins all the cases which go to industrial tribunal. Could it be claimed that this is the result of the training programme? It might be. Alternatively it could be that rising unemployment has made dismissed employees more reluctant to take up cases for fear of being labelled as potential troublemakers by possible new employers. Or the company's increased success rate in tribunal cases could be due to to the increased quality of its representation.

Evaluating Changes in Trainees' Job Behaviour

Managers can be consulted and trainees and trainers can meet in workshops or with individual managers to discuss the effects of training. It is best if this occurs some months after the completion of training so that the full effects can be evaluated. This can act as useful reinforcement for the trainee and can assist trainers to make decisions about modifications to training programmes.

Another useful mechanism is for trainees to be encouraged to compile action plans at end of the programme. The success of training can be evaluated by the degree to which the plan is achieved.

Evaluation by Trainers of their Contribution

It is important that trainers systematically review the extent to which they assisted trainees to meet the objectives of a training programme.

Evaluation at Organizational Level

Relevant indicators include:

- labour turnover rates

- accident rates
- waste of materials
- absenteeism
- productivity

Only thorough investigation is likely to reveal whether improvements in these areas can be attributed to training. Some organizations use a training committee of senior managers to supervise such an assessment.

Feedback of Evaluation Results

To complete the systematic approach to training outlined at the beginning of this chapter, it is vital to feed back the results of evaluation to those involved in the training process.

7 Developing People for the Future

The most obvious categories of employees selected for formal development programmes are those with supervisory or managerial potential or graduate management trainees. Female workers or members of ethnic minority groups may be selected for development as part of the implementation of equal opportunity policies. In this chapter management development is covered in greatest depth, firstly because almost all organizations attempt to develop potential managers and, secondly, because the principles can be applied to other categories of staff.

1 The Focus of Management Development

Prescriptions for the development of effective managers vary greatly. It is superficially simple to implement a 'package' for the off-the-job training of potential managers. It is less easy to develop techniques which match the needs of the particular organization. Nevertheless, it is now largely accepted that the latter approach is more likely to be successful. This is because the requirements for effective management will differ greatly from organization to organization depending on the nature of the market for products and labour, the size of the organization, its history and so on.

A Systematic Approach to Manager Development

To develop a systematic process for the selection and

development of people with potential for managerial positions within five years, it is necessary to answer a number of questions:

- What managerial jobs will we need to fill in five years' time?
- What will be the characteristics (knowledge, skills and personal qualities) of the individuals suitable to fill these positions?
- How can we select some people for development to these positions?
- What training needs do these people have?
- What development programmes can we plan and implement to meet these needs?
- How can we evaluate the process?

The rest of this chapter attempts to answer these questions.

The Link with Human Resource Planning

Answering the first of the questions listed above entails estimating the likely demand for, and supply of, managers in five years' time. The supply of managers in five years' time will be determined by:

- the number in managerial jobs now – by grade, age, job etc.
- retirement over the next five years
- labour turnover over the next five years.

Demand for managers will be influenced by changes in the nature of the business over the next five years – expansion or contraction, for example. Having examined the nature of supply and demand, it will be necessary to:

- examine the degree to which the supply and demand forecasts match
- identify critical shortages or surpluses of labour

- evaluate the options for coping with any mismatch between supply and demand.

Very often it is decided that, if there is likely to be a shortage of managers in the future, the gap should be filled by the development and promotion of existing employees. This is because:

- the characteristics of managerial effectiveness often seem to depend on the particular nature of the organization. Hence employees who 'know the ropes' may be a safer bet than outsiders
- the opportunity of promotion to a managerial position may act as a spur to hard work

Other factors may be the uncertainty and cost of the recruitment and selection process – 'better the devil you know . . .' Information from performance appraisal and personnel records should act as a basis for such judgements. Early identification of potential gives time for systematic development prior to promotion.

Conversely senior management in particular are often externally recruited because an injection of 'new blood' can help ward off stagnation and complacency. There are no easy prescriptions for success in management development. Choice of a strategy should be made after careful consideration of organizational circumstances.

2 Designing Management Development Programmes

The nature of the gap between the characteristics of the potential manager and the requirements of the future job should be delineated as a result of an assessment centre or performance appraisal interview. A development programme must then be designed in the light of individual and organizational circumstances.

Teacher-Centred Approaches

Most managers have experienced some sort of taught management course. The distinction between education and training made in the last chapter is relevant here. Managers need specific skills and knowledge to be effective. Training courses are designed to teach selling techniques, particular areas of legislation, negotiating skills, effective speaking and so on. If well designed and run, these are useful, especially if they give the opportunity for participants to exchange views and experiences with others in similar positions.

Management education specialists argue that managers must be flexible and adaptable to meet the changing circumstances of business organizations. They must be aware of the environmental context – political, social and economic – and able to resolve problems and meet new situations. A variety of post-graduate programmes have been developed to this end. They vary greatly and the intending user should scrutinize a programme carefully prior to enrolment.

Learner-Centred Approaches

While good management teachers assist managers to build positively on their experience, programme content and teaching methods are largely prescribed. There are other approaches to management development which focus on the needs of the learner.

The characteristics of such programmes are:

- the analysis of learning needs and definition of objectives are the responsibilities of the learner
- the learner chooses what to learn and at what pace
- the teacher's role is to support and assist the learning process.

Learner-centred approaches to management develop-

ment are well established. Here we ex
them – action learning and self-managed lea.

Action Learning

This approach is based on the work of Revans, who, after an industrial career, became a professor of management. He felt that taught courses were inappropriate to managers' needs. 'We must give management education back to the managers and let them learn with and from each other during real work.' Thus, action learning programmes have common elements:

- participating managers work on complex and important business problems; the final answers are not known but a series of acceptable next moves might be suggested
- participants 'own' the business problems on which they work and are responsible for implementing a solution
- these managers meet together regularly and on equal terms in 'sets' to report to each other and to discuss problems and progress

'Sets' consisting of four to six participants meet regularly and are assisted by a set adviser. The function of the set is to help participants resolve the business problem which each owns. The set adviser, who may be a teacher, trainer, consultant, personnel specialist or manager, helps set members in a mutual process of giving and receiving help and generally assists with the learning process.

The important difference between this and other management development or research projects is that managers must 'own' the problem on which they work and be able to implement solutions. Revans favours the exchange of participants between organizations, so that a manager experienced in one organizational context is placed in a strange environment. In this way, there is a freshness of approach and a likelihood that organizational conventions will be broken.

Self-Managed Learning

There are many similarities between this approach and action learning; participants are responsible for the management of their learning and there is no predetermined curriculum. Self-managed learning programmes also use 'sets' as a support and progress mechanism.

However, in self-managed learning programmes managers are completely free to analyse their own learning and to choose the associated learning methods in conjunction with set members and staff associated with the programme. The resultant individual programme of study need not be centred on a business problem as in action learning. Rather, participants set their learning objectives following a detailed analysis of their personal characteristics and careers and life objectives. The task is to fulfil the requirements of the individually designed course of study. A variety of learning methods such as attendance at a taught course, guided reading, experiential learning or projects in the workplace or elsewhere may be appropriate.

Management Coaching

Coaching rests on the assumption that someone who has performed a job is qualified to teach a subordinate who aspires to positions of greater responsibility or to better performance in their current role. To be an effective coach the manager must help the subordinate in the identification of development needs and in the methods by which these can be met. Regular coaching sessions should be held to review progress and give further guidance and counselling.

A major advantage of coaching as part of a programme of management development is a close relationship between supervisor and subordinate which should ease problems of integrating new learning with the requirements of present or future jobs.

Not all managers are effective coaches. The characteristics of an effective coach are:

- good communication skills
- willingness to listen and to learn
- a participative style rather than a desire to impose solutions
- interest in the development of more junior employees.

Evaluation of Management Development

It is even more important to review the results of management development activities than other types of training because the per capita expenditure is likely to be higher. The methods used are discussed on pages 87–90. Only by a continuous feedback process can management development activities become closely aligned to organizational needs.

Career Development for Young People

Many organizations plan development programmes for eighteen-year-old school leavers or graduates. Generally, such activities are of two types:

- the 'Cook's tour' of the organization
- specific training in one job.

The 'Cook's tour' involves spending a few months in a number of different departments. The advantage of this approach to career development is that young people learn about various types of work, their relationships with each other and with other parts of the organization.

A further advantage of such an approach is that, done
well, it should assist in the formulation of career goals.
In particular, general management trainees may be able
to decide on the area in which they wish to specialize.

Many young people move straight into permanent
jobs and receive development relevant to their requirements. This may give greater opportunities for the
development of skills in comparison with the 'Cook's
tour', which may give trainees a wide but superficial
knowledge of the organization. Young people in junior
management, technical or professional roles learn by
coping with the demands of their own job rather than
by watching others. In this situation a sympathetic boss
with good coaching skills is vital.

Equal Opportunities in Career Development

As we shall see in Chapter 9, positive action can be
taken to train women or members of ethnic minorities
where it can be shown that they were underrepresented
in particular jobs during the previous year. As yet, relatively few organizations have taken advantage of these
legislation provisions and research has indicated that
fear of resentment from other workers is a major factor.
However, many employers are seeking now to implement equal opportunity policies; as a result, some such
development programmes have been started. A systematic approach to development is vital here, based on
an assessment of both organizational and individual
needs. To assist the planning process, some organizations have set targets for numbers of women and ethnic
minorities to be in particular posts within a certain
period of time.

Employees selected for development in this way are
likely to have occupied relatively routine jobs for many
years in which their capabilities have been underused.
Hence, a helpful component of equal opportunity pro-

grammes may be confidence building and assertiveness training as well as very good facilities for counselling and guidance. The support of managers and other relevant post holders is vital. Some organizations run racism and sexism awareness courses for managers involved in development and promotion decisions to help ensure that career development for minority group employees becomes a reality as part of the implementation of equal opportunity policies.

A Final Word on Development

People are the organization's greatest resource for the future.

A wise counsellor was asked, 'If you had to use a single guide for selecting managers, what would it be?' He replied, 'Tell me what the person does if he wakes up shivering in the middle of the night. If he merely covers his head and hopes the cold will go away, I don't want him. If he climbs out of bed into the cold room and gets another blanket, he has potential.'* We face a similar choice when thinking about managers for the year 2000. We can rely on present practice and hope to get by, or we can treat the pressures ahead as a challenge and devise ways to harness them.

*Managers for the Year 2000, edited by W. L. Newman, Prentice Hall, 1978.

8 Looking After Employees – Welfare and Counselling Services

The development of welfare services in industrial organizations began in the UK in the late nineteenth century, when there was no welfare state and working conditions could be appalling. Some paternalistic employers, most of them Quakers, believed that they had a responsibility to look after their employees for both social and economic reasons.

Most employers still provide welfare services even though it is difficult to prove that these contribute to higher productivity. However, many managers feel that encouraging employees to have a positive attachment both to their jobs and to the employing organization is in the interests of efficiency. Also, being seen as a good employer is likely to be an aid to recruitment. The law emphasizes the need for these services by requiring employers to provide facilities such as wash and rest rooms, adequate lighting, heating and ventilation and fume extraction. As we shall see in the next chapter, the law also lays down statutory minimum rights relevant to employee welfare. Maternity pay and leave fall into this category. State welfare services are geared to the needs of those who do work and increasing unemployment has put strains on them.

1 Definitions of Welfare

The first comprehensive list of the range of personnel management activities to be compiled in Britain was published in 1943. It listed welfare or employee services as:

- Administration of canteen policy
- Sick club and benevolent and saving schemes
- Long service grants
- Pension and superannuation funds or leaving grants
- Granting of loans
- Legal aid
- Advice on individual problems
- Assistance with transport, housing, shopping and other problems
- Provision of social and recreational facilities.

The comprehensive nature of this list was more an expression of pious hope for the future than organizational reality in the immediate postwar period. Now, most large employers do provide specialist welfare services of this sort, though there has been some shift of emphasis from comprehensive state services (housing, transport and recreational provision) towards greater provision of counselling and other personal advice services.

Logically, we would expect that with relatively high unemployment, employers would feel less necessity to provide welfare services to attract or retain staff. However, there is little evidence that such services have been reduced. With technological change, more of the organization's resources tend to be invested in plant and machinery. Hence, payments to employees become a smaller proportion of overall operating costs, and so the provision of welfare services becomes relatively cheaper. As the ratio of capital invested per employee increases, management may become more aware of the need for employees to be fully effective. Welfare services are both cheap and efficient to provide.

The extent of welfare provision depends on management values and policies together with the circumstances of the employing organization. For example, some employers, often paternalistic in outlook, have a policy of peaceful competition with trade unions. This usually involves relatively generous employment policies, including a full and attractive range of welfare services.

2 Personal Services for Employees – Counselling

Most organizations provide employees with counselling or advice services in some or all of these areas:

- Career development
- Legal advice
- Housing
- Bereavement
- Sickness
- Domestic problems
- Retirement
- Redundancy
- Working relationships

Managers or personnel specialists may be called on to help employees in this way but they cannot be called professional counsellors. Few professional counsellors work in the employment field in the UK compared with the United States.

Who Should Undertake Employee Counselling?

The relationship between manager and subordinate often will not be amenable to the development of a counselling relationship. The manager may be concerned with personal status and unwilling or unable to understand the subordinate's position. Also there might be a tendency to protect information which might be useful, such as the employee's REAL prospects of promotion. The employee is likely to find it difficult to seek counselling from the boss. For example, disclosure of domestic problems may hamper promotion prospects.

Specialist personnel staff often take on a counselling role. They may experience fewer problems than line managers. Nevertheless problems of trust and fear of lack of confidentiality so far as employees are concerned do arise. For this reason, some organizations use specialist independent services, staffed by professional counsellors. Even where this is done, both managers and personnel specialists take on the role of counsellor from time to time. In order to carry this out effectively they must be trained.

We have stressed the need for professional individual counselling services, but sometimes non-professional helpers play a very useful role. For example, in career planning, employees can assist each other to identify career and life goals and plan ways of achieving these. In this way mutual support is possible. This is particularly helpful for female employees and members of ethnic minority groups who often fail to achieve their full potential through lack of confidence and skills and a tendency by employers and others to undervalue their abilities. A few employers encourage such counselling as part of equal opportunities programmes.

The Skills of Counselling

It seems that effective counsellors:

- encourage trust from their clients
- relate to their clients
- are people- rather than task-centred
- encourage clients to clarify the situation and to search for their own solutions rather than depending on others

■ supply relevant information but refrain from giving advice.

3 For which Employees may Personnel Welfare Services be Necessary?

Young Employees

Trainees, and employees who have recently completed full-time education, may need special support during the first weeks and months of their employment. Frequently this is provided by those responsible for operating training programmes. Where young people have had to leave home to take a job, employers sometimes provide help with housing.

Those Nearing Retirement

Many employers have encouraged workers nearing retirement age to retire early, as part of a policy to reduce the size of the labour force. For these people and those due to retire at the normal date, it is now common practice to provide retirement counselling and or pre-retirement courses.

Some organizations also provide assistance to retired employees who suffer financial hardship or have personal problems.

Redundant Employees

Redundancy usually comes as a shock to employees. Hence many employers provide similar support to that provided to those nearing retirement, but in addition, advice and assistance on future jobs may be important.

Frequently, at a time of redundancy, attention is focused on those who have to leave, both in terms of financial compensation for loss of jobs and other support services available. Those who continue as employees should not be forgotten. Often they have uncertainties about the future of the organization and their own future within it. Management may need to be particularly vigilant to allay such fears.

The Bereaved and the Sick

Both employees whose close relatives have died and those who have experienced long periods of absence from work because of personal sickness will have financial problems. Personal welfare services can provide advice and assistance.

4 Group Services for Employees

Some employee services are provided for groups rather than individuals. Into this category fall:

- canteen services
- sports and recreational facilities
- facilities for the purchase of goods, in particular those produced or sold by the organization
- occupational health facilities.

Canteen Facilities

Only the smallest organizations tend not to provide any catering facilities for employees. However, canteen facilities can be the most controversial aspect of employee services. As a result, many organizations have canteen committees – a specialist form of joint consultation.

Sports and Social Facilities

Welfare services for employees originated at the end of the nineteenth century, when provision of state services in this general area was sparser than today. Many paternalistic employees opened sports and social clubs for employees and their families. Today not only has provision by local authorities increased, but the recreational and social habits of the population changed. Many employees like to spend their leisure time away from premises provided by the employer. Some employers have kept their facilities but have made them more open to the public at large.

Facilities for the Purchase of Goods

Some companies run 'staff shops' where goods produced by the employer or associated employers can be purchased at a discount and provide facilities for personal services, such as banking or hairdressing.

Occupational Health Facilities

Each year about 350 million working days are lost through sickness and industrial injuries. In most years this is over thirty times the working days lost through strikes. It makes economic sense for employers to provide occupational health services for employees. In Europe such services are usually a legal requirement. The aims of an occupational health service are:

- to assist in the establishment and maintenance of the highest possible physical and mental health of employees
- to ensure the employees' health allows them to cope with their jobs
- to protect employees from any health hazard which may arise from their jobs

The interpretation of such aims differs from one organization to another. Where the nature of the work is inherently hazardous, more attention is given to the provision of occupational health services.

Many employers see occupational health provision as an educational or preventive service and therefore may include medical screening on smoking, alcohol and diet. Increasing attention is being given to work-related stress.

Status Considerations

In the UK it has been customary to stratify employee services provision and fringe benefits according to the status of employees. This is a reflecton of our class structure. Recently employers have moved towards single status for all employees, though often this excludes senior management who retain the rights to 'top-hat' pension schemes, separate car parks and other symbols of position.

Differences in the provision of employee benefits and facilities have been a source of discontent. Yet moves to 'single staff status' may also be a cause of grievance for higher-grade employees who resent the loss of status differentials. Change in this area needs careful handling by management usually in consultation or negotiation with trade unions.

The Future of Employee Services

Two trends likely to affect the provision of employee services in the next five years are:

- State welfare provision is unlikely to improve and may decline further. Employers may feel a responsibility to fill gaps in state provision for their employees
- As organizations become more capital intensive, i.e. as the amount of financial investment per employee increases, it becomes relatively cheaper to provide a full range of employee services.

9 The Law and the Rights of the Individual Employee

One of the complexities of employment law is that the length of service required before workers acquire particular legal rights varies quite considerably. The following checklist summarizes the current position.

1 Checklist of Individual Employment Rights

When Someone Applies for a Job, They are Protected from:

- race and sex discrimination
- the 'need' to declare 'spent' offences.

On Starting Work, Employees are Entitled to:

- protection against dismissal or other unfavourable treatment on grounds of race, sex or trade union activity
- equal pay (for both men and women)
- paid time off for antenatal care
- paid time off for trade union duties*
- time off for trade union activities*
- time off for public duties*
- an itemized pay statement*
- monetary compensation if the employer fails to give the necessary statutory notice in cases of redundancy
- monetary compensation if the employer becomes insolvent
- statutory sick pay provided that they earn more than the 'lower earnings limit'.

With Service, Employees Accrue Additional Rights, as Follows:

After 4 weeks:

- a minimum period of notice
- guarantee payments and protection from dismissal, if the employer cannot provide work
- monetary compensation and protection from dismissal, if the employer suspends workers on certain medical grounds.

After 13 weeks:

- written particulars of the contract of employment

After 26 weeks:

- a written statement of the reasons for dismissal

After 2 years:

- protection from unfair dismissal
- maternity pay
- maternity leave
- redundancy compensation
- paid time off to look for work in cases of redundancy.

Most of the rights listed here apply to full-time workers, part-time workers who work more than 16 hours per week and part-timers who work more than 8 hours a week and have at least 5 years' continuous service. Those asterisked (above) apply only to those who work 16 hours a week or more.

In this chapter we focus on the major legal rights of employees other than those associated with the termination of the contract of employment.

2 Anti-Discrimination Legislation and Employee Rights

Promotion Opportunities

In the same way as they must not discriminate against applicants for employment, employers must give equal opportunities for transfer and promotion.

For example, in 1979 nearly half of the 900 platform staff employed by Bradford Metro, the public bus company service in Bradford, West Yorkshire, were of Asian origin. Many of them had ten to fifteen years' service. There were no Asian inspectors and only one West Indian inspector out of fifty people employed in this capacity. An investigation by the Commission for Racial Equality (CRE) revealed that the district manager instructed interviewers to be cautious in appointing Asian inspectors. Reasons given for this included fear of opposition from white busmen and problems with the travelling public. As a result, higher standards of performance, including those required in a written test, were demanded of Asian applicants.

The CRE in its investigation, found that Asian applicants did disproportionately badly; the instructions to interviewers were directly discriminatory; the test was indirectly discriminatory since it did not measure relevant abilities and the standard of English demanded was not necessary for effective job performance. The company should devise a more appropriate test.

Other actions taken by Bradford Metro since the CRE investigation include:

- the introduction of an equal opportunities policy
- a programme of language training for Asian busmen to improve their chances of promotion
- training for managers and supervisors in a multi-racial workforce.

A higher proportion of Asians and West Indians are now inspectors.

Training

Legislation protects employees who believe themselves to have been denied equal opportunity for training. In addition, the Sex Discrimination Act and the Race Relations Act include positive discrimination provisions, where during the previous year there were no (or comparatively few) persons of one sex or race doing a particular type of work. In such circumstances the provisions of special training programmes is permissible. This is the only legal provision for positive discrimination in the UK at present. Once members of minority groups have received training, they must be selected for jobs on merit alone.

Benefits, Facilities and Services

Employers must give equal access to fringe benefits to all their employees. Thus it would be illegal for a bank to offer low-cost mortgages to male employees only.

The Equality Commissions

The Equal Opportunities Commission (EOC) and the Commission for Racial Equality (CRE) are charged with the identification and elimination of obstacles to the achievement of equality of opportunity for women and members of ethnic minorities. Their members and employees operate independently of government, though they are paid by the state. They must keep relevant legislation under review and, where necessary, suggest amendments. They also promote research and educational activities. The Commissions have drawn up codes of practice on the elimination of unfair discrimination. These are not legally binding but are admissible in evidence before an industrial tribunal or court. Both Commissions can conduct formal investigations, either on their own initiative or at the request of the Secretary of State for Employment. Where evidence of unlawful discrimination is found, non-discrimination notices can be issued to prevent further discrimination.

Equal Pay

The Equal Pay Act is also concerned with unfair discrimination at work. Broadly, it deals with wages and other terms and conditions of employment whereas the Sex Discrimination Act covers the terms of an offer of employment and is concerned with the elimination of discrimination in recruitment, training, promotion and other aspects of the employment relationship.

The Equal Pay Act gives all workers, both male and female, the right to equal treatment in individual contracts of employment. It also provides for references to be made to the Central Arbitration Committee, which can amend discriminatory collective agreements or employers' pay structures. In order for such changes to be made by the committee, these must contain clauses which refer only to men or to women. Here we shall discuss the law as if we were dealing with a woman's claim for equal pay.

Claims under the Equal Pay Act

It is up to the applicant for equal pay to select a comparator in order to make a claim. The comparator must be employed by the same or an associated employer and normally he must work at the same place as her and be employed under the same terms and conditions of employment. It is possible to make a comparison with a predecessor but only if he occupied the job recently.

Having found a man with whom to compare herself, the employee must be able to show that she is employed:

  ■ on 'like work' to that of a man

or
- in a job which, though different from that of a man, has been rated as equivalent under a job evaluation scheme

or
- under the Equal Pay Act (Amendment) Regulations, on work of equal value to a man's in terms of the demands on her under such headings as effort, skill and decision-making; in such cases there need not be a job evaluation scheme or, where there is, she can claim that it has discriminatory results.

'Like Work'

'Like work' is defined by the Act as being of 'the same or broadly similar nature' to the man's work. The courts have said that tribunals need not undertake a minute examination of the differences between the work done by the woman and that done by the man. For example, a cook who prepared meals for an executive dining room compared her work with that of an assistant chef in the works canteen. Differences in the hours worked and in the volume and nature of the meals prepared, were felt to be insufficient justification for unequal pay. That is, they were not of 'practical importance'.

The points which tribunals consider to determine whether differences are of practical importance are:

- the nature of the differences
- whether they occur in practice
- how often they occur
- whether the differences are sufficiently significant to justify differences in terms and conditions of employment.

Some tribunals have used as a yardstick whether two men would be paid differently if they did the jobs in question.

Work 'Rated as Equivalent'

This is a very limited point of access to equal pay for most women. First, the organization concerned must have a job evaluation scheme and both the woman's job and that of the man with whom she chooses to compare herself must be covered by it. Surveys suggest that, while the majority of large employers use such techniques, many small ones do not. Secondly, an examination of legal judgements reveals that, once job evaluation schemes have been designed and implemented, it is very difficult to challenge them, unless it can be shown that there has been a failure to apply the scheme in accordance with its rules.

'Equal Pay for Work of Equal Value'

Because the UK is a member of the European Economic Community, its legislation can be challenged in the European Court of Justice. In 1982 this court ruled that because the Equal Pay Act does not entitle a woman to claim equal pay for work of equal value unless her employer uses a job evaluation scheme, UK legislation failed to comply with EEC law. As a result the Equal Pay Act has been amended. A woman who cannot achieve equal pay by either of the routes described above may achieve it if a tribunal considers that her job is of 'equal value' to that of the man with whom she compares herself. This route can be used where there is no job evaluation scheme or where the woman wishes to challenge an existing job evaluation scheme as discriminatory. Comparisons may be made between jobs covered by different evaluation schemes or pay structures. Independent experts approved by ACAS are used by tribunals to determine whether the two jobs are of equal value.

Genuine Material Differences

Even where the tribunal agrees that two jobs are 'broadly similar', 'rated as equivalent under a job evaluation scheme' or of 'equal value', the employer can avoid equal pay by proving that there is a 'genuine material difference' between them. For example, if the woman has less experience than the man or is younger than him and these are relevant factors in determining pay, then it would be reasonable in law to pay less to the woman than to the man. For equal value claims the employee must show that the difference in pay is due to sex discrimination.

3 Maternity Rights Legislation

Maternity Leave

A woman who has two years' continuous service by the eleventh week before her baby is due has the right to return to work after the birth, provided she:

- gives 21 days' notice in writing of resignation due to pregnancy, states the intention to return and gives the date when the baby is expected
- confirms within 14 days that she still intends to return to work in reply to a letter from her employer 49 days after the date when the baby is due
- gives her employer at least 21 days' notice of her intention to return to work.

Normally women return to work 29 weeks after the baby's birth. They are not prevented by law from telling the employer that they intend to return and then changing their mind once the baby is born.

The employer must allow the woman to return to her previous job unless it is not 'reasonably practicable'. In such cases she must be offered suitable alternative work, i.e. the terms and conditions of employment must not be substantially less favourable than they would have been, had she gone back to her previous job.

Maternity Pay

The service and notice requirements for maternity pay are the same as for maternity leave. Maternity pay is normally nine tenths of the weekly wage. The employer must make the payment but can reclaim it in full from the state maternity fund.

Paid Time off for Antenatal Care

Pregnant women can have a reasonable amount of time off for antenatal care provided that, on request, they show proof both of pregnancy and of the date and time of appointments.

4 Other Rights to Time Off from Work

Time Off for Trade Union Duties

Representatives of unions recognized by the employer for collective bargaining purposes have the right to reasonable paid time off for industrial relations duties in the organization in which they work. This includes:

- collective bargaining with management
- communicating with members about such negotiations
- consulting full-time officers
- dealing with members' grievances and disciplinary cases
- attending relevant training courses.

Safety representatives also have rights to paid time off to perform their functions.

Time Off for Trade Union Activities

Union members have the right to unpaid time off to take part in the activities of the union. Such activities include:

- attending a conference as a union delegate
- attending union meetings
- voting in union elections.

There is no right to time off for anything connected with industrial action.

Clarification of these legal provisions can be found in the ACAS Code of Practice, *Time Off for Trade Union Duties and Activities*.

Time Off for Public Duties

Employees are entitled to reasonable unpaid time off to perform the following duties:

- justice of the peace
- member of a local authority
- member of any statutory tribunal
- member of a health authority
- member of the governing body of any educational establishment maintained by a local education authority
- member of a water authority
- jury service
- member of the voluntary reserve forces.

Sick Pay and Medical Suspension

Employers are responsible for the payment of earnings related statutory sick pay (SSP) for the first eight weeks of sickness. The full amount of such payments can be recouped from the state. However, many employees have contractual rights to sick pay which exceed these payments. The regulations governing SSP are complex and detailed.

Suspension from Work on Medical Grounds

Workers whose health has been put at risk by exposure to hazardous substances must be taken off their normal jobs and offered suitable alternative work. Otherwise, they may be suspended on full pay for up to six months. There are detailed regulations covering this aspect of employment. However, the number of employees covered is small.

Payments to Workers when there is no Work to do

Management has no right to suspend employees, cut their rates of pay, introduce short-time working or lay them off unless this is provided for in their contracts of employment. Many union agreements provide for guaranteed minimum earnings during a period of lay off. In addition, workers are entitled to small minimum 'guarantee payments' for days when no work is provided. Frequently, collective agreements provide for higher payments.

The Limits of Employment Law

Since 1963, when employees gained the right to minimum periods of notice, there has been a vast increase in employee rights legislation. However, much of the relationship between management and employees is untouched by law. For example, the UK is the only EEC country apart from Denmark which has no general legislation on hours of work. Nor is there legislation

fixing the length of holidays. There is no minimum
wage legislation, though some workers do have their
wages fixed by wages councils. This is not so for all low
paid workers and in many cases the statutory minimum
rates laid down by wages councils are very low indeed.
There has been opposition to a national minimum wage
and other minimum terms and conditions of employment because of the fear that additional unemployment
could result. This is debatable.

10   Fair Pay and Employee Benefits at Work

While there are motivations other than money, pay is a major factor in the employment relationship. It is management's task to find the package of inducements which prompts maximum employee productivity. To be effective, this package must fit particular organizational circumstances and be reviewed regularly.

1 Factors Affecting Salary and Wage Levels

Pay levels reflect the rate for labour in the external 'market'. Internal organizational factors mainly associated with the establishment and maintenance of pay differentials, and individual factors associated with performance and commitment as demonstrated by length of service or 'merit', for example. The level of pay can be seen as the result of the interaction between management's desire to obtain maximum employee productivity for minimum cost and employees' wishes for the highest possible reward for the least effort. For this reason the contractual relationship between employer and employee is sometimes termed the wage-effort bargain – see figure 10.

In this sense, rewards may be money, status, a sense of achievement and so on. It is important for management to recognize that not all employees expect the same reward. In designing wage and salary administration policies, management should be aware of the complexity of this aspect of employment relationship.

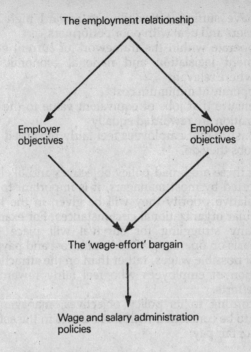

Figure 10. The wage-effort bargain

Wage and Salary Administration Policies

Management should be clear about its objectives in this area before thinking through appropriate policies. Some possible objectives for management with regard to remuneration are to:

- attract suitable employees
- encourage effective employees to remain in the organization
- obtain optimal performance from employees
- encourage employees to improve their performance

- have sufficient flexibility to reward high performers and deal with poor performers
- operate within the framework of current employment legislation and national economic policy where relevant
- operate at minimum cost
- ensure that jobs of equivalent value to the organization are rewarded equally
- ensure that employees feel fairly rewarded for the jobs they do.

While these are broad policy objectives and likely to be supported by most managers, it is important to assess the relative priority they will be given in the light of particular organizational circumstances. For example, a company struggling for survival will place greater emphasis on operating at minimum cost and paying the lowest possible wages, rather than on the attraction and retention of employees who feel fairly rewarded for their efforts.

According to its policy objectives, management is likely to be concerned with three issues in the establishment of fair pay:

- wage or salary relativities – to ensure that what is paid is fair in comparison with payments received by other employees within the organization
- to ensure that pay is fair in comparison with other employers
- methods of payment which encourage effective performance and commitment by individuals or work groups.

This can be expressed diagramatically – see figure 11.

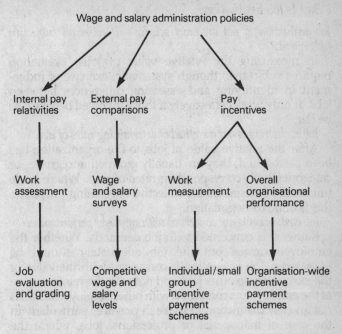

Figure 11. *Wage and salary administration policies and practices*

2 Job Evaluation and The Design of Pay Structures

Bernard Shaw in 'Everybody's Political What's What' challenged the possibility of being able to 'assess in pounds, shillings and pence the difference between the social service of an archbishop and a turfbookmaker or to fix a just wage for poets laureate and sausage makers'. Job evaluation attempts to establish the relative value of jobs to the employing organization. In the UK there has been no attempt to undertake a national exercise of the type required to meet Shaw's challenge.

What Is Job Evaluation?

Job evaluation is not an exact science — it relies on subjective judgement.

In measuring the relative value of jobs, evaluation requires subjective, though systematic, exercise of judgement in identifying and assessing differences between jobs. It only works effectively if those involved believe it to be fair.

Job evaluation is not a method of determining rates of pay.

After the relative value of jobs to the organization has been established, they are usually grouped into grades or categories with corresponding rates of pay. Where trade unions are recognized for collective bargaining purposes, this is done by negotiation.

Job evaluation is not concerned with employee performance.

Rather it is concerned with job demands. Whether the employee carries out the job adequately should be immaterial. Job evaluation is concerned with the value of the job relative to other jobs and not with the relative value of the employee as compared with other employees. This is not an easy distinction to make in practice, particularly in the case of managerial or professional jobs, where the individual, to some degree, defines the nature of the tasks performed. Nevertheless, for job evaluation purposes, it is important to attempt the distinction.

In sum, job evaluation attempts to answer three questions critical to the management of people:

- What is the relative value of a job to the organization?
- How can this value be determined?
- How can this be done in a way that is accepted as fair by most employees?

The Process of Job Evaluation

Figure 12 emphasizes the basic steps to be followed in evaluating jobs.

Job analysis

Job description

Select benchmark
jobs

Job evaluation

Job grading

Pay determination

Figure 12. The process of job evaluation

In Chapter 2 we discussed job analysis and writing job descriptions. To encourage employees to believe in the fairness of the results of job evaluation, care must be taken at this stage to involve them or their representatives. This can be achieved as follows:

- Employees can be asked to complete questionnaires on the demands of their jobs. These can be accompanied by a job description. Both job holder and manager should sign to indicate that the information presented is accurate.
- Job holders can be interviewed by a job analyst and information on job demands is compiled for signature as above.
- Job holders can be observed at work by analysts who again compile information. This may be suitable

only for manual jobs where activities are directly observable.

In medium or large organizations it is usual to select a sample (ten to thirty) of 'benchmark' jobs at this stage as a basis for the establishment of the job evaluation system. Such jobs should be:

- well known to the evaluators
- representative of the level and type of jobs to be evaluated
- not the subject of a dispute between management and employees.

Now job evaluation can take place. This will result in the establishment of a rank order of jobs in the organization. These then can be grouped into grades. Only then is the pay for grades established either by negotiation or by managerial judgement.

3 Methods of Job Evaluation

There are two main ways of evaluating jobs – analytical and non-analytical. Analytical methods break down jobs into their constituent parts for assessment purposes; non-analytical methods evaluate jobs as wholes.

Non-Analytical Methods

Job ranking. This is the simplest method of job evaluation. There is no analysis other than the overall decision of the evaluators about the relative value of each job.

Suppose that this rank order of four jobs is established by job ranking:

- electrician
- cook

- kitchen assistant
- cleaner

The most obvious problem of putting this result into practice is the absence of any indication as to how much more important one job is than the next in the hierarchy. So this can be a very blunt and biased evaluation tool. Its results may be questioned. It may be inappropriate to the needs of a very small company, however.

Paired comparisons. This is a form of job ranking but with an element of scoring which measures a job's importance in relation to others, so producing a final league table of jobs. Again, this non-analytical method tends to be used in small companies, though it can be used to obtain a ranking of benchmark jobs in larger ones.

Job classification. This involves the categorization of jobs within broadly defined grades. It is used in the Civil Service and in teaching. Once the number of grades to be used has been determined, a general job description for each grade is prepared. Here is an example:

- Level 3
  Tasks calling for independent arrangement of work and exercise of some initiative, where supervision is needed. Detailed familiarity with one or more branches of established procedure required.

This definition is rather broad; quite different responsibilities could be grouped within it. Yet, in certain circumstances, it may be too rigid, leading to exclusion of jobs on seemingly trivial grounds. Recently some companies have moved to more analytical schemes because these problems have made it difficult to encompass rapid changes in technology and the attendant more complex job descriptions. On the other hand, job classification systems are simple and cheap to administer.

Analytical Methods

Jobs are assessed under a number of headings such as decision making, working conditions and knowledge required. By comparing total numerical values, assessors can gauge the relative value of jobs to the organization; very different jobs can be compared.

Points rating. This method enables evaluators to give a points score to each job. There is no standardized points system suitable for all organizations.

Stages of designing and implementing a points rating system.

1 Establish a representative committee. It is common for schemes to be designed and implemented by joint management-union working groups to ensure that the results of job evaluation are perceived as fair.

2 Analyse a significant sample of jobs and write job descriptions. Benchmark jobs should be selected according to the criteria listed on p.126.

3 Select and define those criteria considered most critical in determining differences between jobs. This is difficult. Too many factors make the scheme over complex and lead to elements of jobs being counted twice, so that the objectivity of the scheme is cast in doubt. Too few factors make it difficult to cover the full range of jobs effectively. It is helpful to look at schemes used in the same industry or for similar occupational groups when designing a scheme. Great care must be taken to define each factor so that it can be applied to each job covered by the scheme.

4 Weight factors and convert to points. Commonly certain factors have a higher number of points allocated than others, reflecting the relative importance attached to a particular factor. Here is a list of factors which the joint management-union working group in Colin's Cars, a manufacturer of sports cars, has

decided should be used to evaluate all non-manual jobs in the company:

- education
- experience
- specialized knowledge
- complexity of task
- communication – contacts and relationships
- management of people
- supervision received
- physical environment.

The next task is to attach weights to the factors. For this evaluators need an intimate knowledge of the value placed on particular jobs in Colin's Cars and the reasons for this. There are no universally correct weightings; the right ones are those which ultimately produce an acceptable ranking of jobs.

After weights have been allocated, each factor definition will have to be sub-divided into degrees or levels. Below are the factor and sub-factor definitions for 'specialized knowledge' in the scheme being designed for use in Colin's Cars:

Specialized knowledge (weighting eight per cent).
This factor appraises the degree to which it is essential for the job holder to have specialized knowledge.

Level
1 No specialized knowledge required.
2 Some specialized knowledge or understanding of techniques and terminology to a working standard.
3 A higher level of specialized knowledge of understanding of techniques and terminology to a working standard.
4 A good 'in-depth' level of specialized knowledge or understanding of techniques and terminology so that some guidance and interpretation may be given to others.

5 Specialized knowledge and techniques associated with the job are required to be understood in great depth and detail so that available information can not only be well understood and interpreted but also translated into instructions for the guidance of others.

In points rating schemes it is quite common for a total of 500 points to be used. Thus a maximum of forty points would be allocated to 'specialized knowledge' in this example.

5 Test run a selection of jobs. The benchmark jobs are evaluated using the newly designed scheme.
6 Compare with the established hierarchy of jobs. It cannot be stressed too often that job evaluation schemes only work effectively if the results are acceptable to employees. It is necessary to assess the likelihood of the system producing acceptable results. To do this, the points allocated to each job in the test run are plotted against rates currently paid to job holders – see figure 13.

A line of 'best fit' can be drawn through the points indicating those jobs which are out of line. In this table jobs A and B are out of line and are known as 'red circle' and 'green circle' jobs respectively. Job A is overpaid and job B is underpaid, since in theory the introduction of the job evaluation scheme should be self-financing in that the cost of bringing green circle jobs up to the line of best fit should be balanced by the savings derived from reducing the pay associated with red circle jobs.

Usually there is a 'buying-in' cost; the wages bill will increase at the time the new scheme is introduced. Normally the pay of red circle jobs is frozen until cost-of-living increases catch up with them. Holders of green circle jobs may be given pay increases.

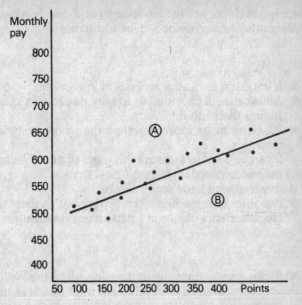

Figure 13. Scattergram of the relationship between points and existing pay levels

7 Adjust factor weights and points. There may not be such a good fit between points and pay as that indicated in figure 13. In this case, stages 5, 6 and 7 may have to be repeated until an acceptable result is obtained.

8 Evaluate all jobs. The remaining jobs should fall close to the line of best fit which has already been established. Red circle and green circle jobs will have to be dealt with as indicated above.

9 Divide the jobs into grades. The points scores are a basis for determining the grades which will encompass groups of similar jobs. Careful thought must be given to both the break points between the grades and the numbers of grades.

Here is a summary of the advantages and disadvantages of the points rating method of job evaluation:

Advantages

- It encourages careful analysis of job content
- A rationale is provided as to why one job is graded higher than another
- It seems to be more objective than non-analytical methods
- It can be used to measure the value of new jobs and thus accommodate technological change
- It can cover a wide range of jobs
- A points rating scheme can be devised to meet the characteristics of jobs in a particular organization.

Disadvantages

- It can give a spurious impression of mathematical accuracy. Like all job evaluation methods, it is subjective.
- It is time-consuming and therefore expensive, particularly if a large number of factors are used.
- In practice, it is difficult to make a points rating system cover a very wide range of jobs – from managerial to manual, for example – because of the difficulty of weighting factors where one set of factors may be more relevant to one category of jobs than another.
- To be seen to be fair, management (and trade unions where relevant) may wish to give employees information about the system. This is likely to lead to problems, for example in justifying factor weightings.

In conclusion, points rating is probably the most popular method of job evaluation.

Checklist of Questions for Management and Personnel Specialists Contemplating the Introduction of Job Evaluation

- Which method should we use?
- Should we use management consultants and if so in what capacity?
- Which categories of employees do we want the scheme to cover?
- Will more than one scheme be needed to cover all employees?
- Shall we involve trade unions or other employee representatives? If so, to what extent?
- What shall be the constitution of any working group needed to design the scheme?
- Who will be the job evaluators and what training will they need?
- What training will managers and union representatives, other than those directly involved, need?
- Who will do all this training?
- How much information about job evaluation should we communicate to employees?
- What mechanism should we use to review the scheme to ensure that once implemented it works effectively?

4 External Pay Comparisons

There is no market rate 'for a job', rather there is a range of rates paid by different employers, either because the duties performed, even where the job title is the same, vary somewhat or because wage and salary policies of employers differ, as suggested on pp. 120–124.

Market Rate Surveys

It will be necessary to use market surveys to develop

and maintain competitive salary and wage structures. Examples of such surveys are:

- Company surveys – sometimes companies form a 'club' for the exchange of this sort of information
- General published surveys – these usually give information by industrial sector, size of organization and job title. Sometimes information on employee benefits is also included
- Specialized surveys – these are carried out by professional bodies, trade unions and employers' or trade associations
- It is also possible to obtain similar information from an analysis of job advertisements – this information is more problematic than the other sources since job descriptions may be 'glossy' to attract candidates and salary data is often incomplete or inflated.

The skill is to extract a market rate for a job which is a reasonable compromise between all available data. In making such judgements, the following questions will be helpful:

- Does the survey show a single rate or a range for a particular job?
- When was it carried out? Has it been updated since?
- Is the sample sufficiently large to be representative of the organizations, jobs, locations and so on required?
- Is the pay data comparable, i.e. are overtime, shift pay and other additions to normal earnings clearly indicated?
- Is information available on employee benefits?
- Are job descriptions available and not just job titles?
- For what purpose is the information produced – as a service or to exchange information? Are there

other purposes, for example consultants attempting to attract clients?
- Is the information clear and easy to understand?
- Is the survey value for money?

5 Salary and Wage Administration

Internal pay relativities can be established by job evaluation and related to the external market for labour by the use of wage and salary surveys. Final pay levels will then be established either by managerial judgement or by negotiation with recognized trade unions. With manual jobs, this may be the end of the story, since there is likely to be a rate for the job regardless of length of service or performance. For non-manual workers it is more likely that, for each grade of job, there will be an associated salary range with a minimum rate of pay. Progression through grades may be entirely on the basis of managerial judgement of 'merit' or automatically with length of service. Trade unions have tended to prefer the latter method since it restricts the prerogative of management to show favouritism. Very often there is an overlap between the salary range associated with one grade and that of adjacent grades. The rationale for this is that an employee with much experience in a new job at one level is worth more to the organization than a new recruit to a job in the grade above.

A further design feature of salary structures to which management should give attention is the width of the grade bands. Broad bands emphasize the performance of the individual within the grade whereas narrow bands place more importance on the level of the job and on promotion from one category to another. In many organizations, narrow grade bands are more common for junior staff, recognizing that there are limited variations in performance at this level. For more senior staff, broad bands are needed for the recognition of individual responsibility. Sometimes there is provision to pay exceptional staff more than the top of the salary scale of the grade in which their job falls.

Pay Incentives

Job evaluation is used frequently to give a structure for basic pay. However, other pay elements are often added to this. One of the most common, for production employees in particular, has tended to be incentive payments directly related to the effort expended by the individual or the work group.

6 Payment by Results

The incentive element in these payment systems normally comprises no more than twenty-five per cent of the pay packet and this proportion is tending to decline as a proportion of total earnings. This is because, as much manual work has become subject to technological change, it has become more machine paced. As a result, the individual employee has a decreasing ability to affect the amount of production. In these circumstances payment by results becomes less appropriate.

The Mechanics of Payment by Results Systems

Work study or management services specialists play a prominent role in the operation of most payment by results systems. These rest on the concept of a 'standard time' – the time necessary for an appropriately qualified operator to complete a clearly defined task at an acceptable level of quality. Time standards are established through the systematic application of work measurement techniques.

Payment by results systems are used primarily in situations where:

- work cycles are generally short and repetitive
- output can be measured in terms of units produced
- work has a high labour content and is not predominantly machine paced
- high-quality production is not essential
- jobs are relatively stable
- sufficient back-up stocks are available to meet fluctuations in both demand and output.

This is important because payment by results systems give employees considerable control over output. If they wish to limit production, either for individual or group reasons, they can do so. Also, employees are likely to become very discontented if their bonus earnings are reduced by shortages of components.

Other conditions for the successful introduction of payment by results systems are that:

- cooperation is forthcoming from employees who are not able to participate in the bonus scheme
- high bonus earnings of individuals or groups will not stimulate pressure for parity from other employees
- sufficient well-trained work study or management services specialists are employed.

Assumptions Behind Payment by Results

Work-study-based payment systems, like job evaluation, are systematic rather than scientific techniques. They are based on the assessment of production times and work as incentives only if all concerned believe them to be fair. They are designed on the assumption that the 'carrot' of more pay will encourage workers to greater output. This is controversial; whilst money is an important source of motivation, it is not the only one for all workers at all times.

Research on the effect of incentive payments suggests the following problems may occur.

Bargaining over rates. Work study and management services techniques are subjective though systematic. Some jobs are 'tightly' timed whilst others have loose times. It is much more beneficial for the employee to have 'loose' times. Thus, there is likely to be bargaining both over work allocation and the times allocated to jobs.

Work group pressure to keep production down. Employees whose output is much higher than the norm are often under pressure to reduce their productivity; very high output by an individual can endanger bonus earnings in that management may come to believe that all are capable of more effort and may reduce the rate accordingly.

Employees' dislike of fluctuating earnings. Employees attempt to create stabilizing devices which may distort management's assessment of output.

Payment by results systems, then, can have disadvantageous effects on workplace industrial relations.

7 Measured Daywork Systems

These are often introduced to overcome the disadvantages of both payment by results and payment by time. Pay is fixed at a higher level than for time-rated work on the understanding that a standard performance is achieved and maintained. Pay does not fluctuate in the short term with actual performance. If an employee consistently fails to achieve the required standard even after further help and training, a wide range of sanctions are applied – withdrawal or reduction of bonus and ultimately dismissal.

The advantages of measured daywork compared with payment by results systems include:

- the avoidance of the industrial relations problems often associated with payment by results systems whilst retaining an incentive element
- a strong sanction against poor performance
- probably less resistance to changes in working methods since earnings will not be affected
- a greater potential for employee cooperation and flexibility because bonus paid is the same for any job
- greater control over wages costs
- lower administrative costs since bonus is standard and only exceptions are calculated
- a positive incentive to training to maintain bonus earnings.

On the other hand, measured daywork requires closer and better supervision than payment by results and a steady workflow and effective monitoring of the system. In addition, some organizations which have changed from payment by results to measured daywork, have experienced at least a short-term fall in productivity.

8 Plant and Organization-wide Incentive Schemes, Profit Sharing and Share Ownership

The most common of these schemes are:

Added value schemes. Added value equals sales revenue less expenditure on materials and services purchased outside the organization. An increase in added value above a given norm represents an improvement in performance which can be shared with employees according to an agreed formula.

Profit sharing schemes. These involve the distribution

of either shares or cash from company profits in a pre-specified way to employees.

In the past there has been a lack of interest in these approaches to payment in the UK. The reasons for this probably include:

- employees' difficulty in relating their individual efforts to the amount of bonus received
- a low commitment by workers to the 'free enterprise society'.

However, there has been an upsurge of interest in these systems recently – particularly in profit sharing, which has been encouraged by government tax concessions. One reason for this may be that organizations are becoming more capital intensive and work is becoming more machine paced. As a result, it is more difficult to design effective payment by results or even measured daywork systems. Yet, to retain or increase competitiveness, incentives are vital.

9 Fair Benefits at Work

So far we have examined monetary remuneration. In Chapter 8 we discussed employee services such as sports and canteen facilities. Other non-monetary benefits or services relate to the termination of employment and are discussed in Chapter 11. Other benefits sometimes provided are company cars, medical and life assurance and relocation allowances. Management should determine its policy on employee benefits as part of its overall remuneration policy.

What of the Future?

In Chapter 7 we identified a trend towards harmonization in terms and conditions of employment. Some writers predict this may also occur in payment and job evaluation systems as more employees are white- rather than blue-collar and as it becomes increasingly necessary to justify differences between men and women because of equal pay legislation. Petty and unjustified differences in rewards are likely to offend employees. Equity between levels of tasks is vital to generate a sense of fairness in pay and benefits.

11 Dismissal, Redundancy and Retirement

To deal effectively with disciplinary matters and dismissal, managers and personnel specialists need:

- a knowledge of employment legislation
- an understanding of the organization's disciplinary procedures
- an awareness of the way similar cases have been dealt with in their own organization and elsewhere. Personnel specialists usually play a coordinating and advisory role here
- skills in dealing with disciplinary cases.

1 Discipline Handling Skills

The object of disciplinary interviews is to modify the offending employee's behaviour so that it more closely accords with the organization's requirements. Whilst the possibility of sanctions is ever present, the focus should be on problem solving. It is vital that employees are given an opportunity to explain their behaviour if any subsequent dismissal is to be considered fair. Also, management will wish to ensure that the malaise does not spread. For example, persistent latecomers who escape scot-free are likely to be a source of discontent to other employees. Justice must not only be done; it must be seen to be done.

Managers normally initiate disciplinary interviews to establish the full facts of the situation and to issue a rebuke if necessary.

Preparation for Disciplinary Interviewing

To conduct a disciplinary interview effectively, managers need knowledge of the following:

- the job – nature of the duties and standard of work required
- the working environment – physical conditions of work, working relationships
- the employee's work record and circumstances – information on past performance, behaviour and circumstances both in work and outside where relevant to the cases

Having established the facts of the situation, managers also must acquaint themselves with possible available sanctions. Only with adequate preparation is it possible to conduct an effective disciplinary interview.

Participants in Disciplinary Interviews

Managers will need to consider whether they wish to conduct disciplinary interviews alone or with a personnel specialist. Some procedure agreements specify the point at which the latter should become involved. If such guidance is not available, it will be necessary to consider the degree of formality advisable in the circumstances. Employees have the right to be represented either by union representatives or by colleagues in these circumstances. Again, the presence of others is likely to increase formality. To guard themselves against later accusations of unfairness, managers should inform employees of their right to be represented. The presence of a union representative should not be feared; very often this acts as additional insurance that the employee will carry out any promises of improved future performance or behaviour.

The Interview Itself

The initiative for the interview comes from management. First, there should be an attempt to establish the full facts both by explaining what information is held and by asking for the employee's comments. Forcing a confession by attempting to place the individual under considerable stress or preaching a sermon is unlikely to contribute to correction of the problem. A more constructive approach is to try to agree how improvement can be achieved. Such a problem-solving approach will be assisted by the judicious use of questions.

The categories of questions used in discussion of the selection interview in Chapter 2, pages 27–30, can be applied to disciplinary interviewing. The most obviously useful are open and probing questions to establish the employee's perception of the situation. Linking statements or questions should also be used to ensure that the interview is a conversation with a purpose. Indirect questions may be useful in further assisting understanding of the case.

Follow Up of Disciplinary Interviews

It is important to keep an accurate record of the interview both to ensure that agreements are kept and in case the situation is not rectified and the employee is subsequently dismissed. New facts which have come to light during the interview will need to be checked. The employee's subsequent behaviour and performance must be carefully monitored to determine whether further disciplinary action is necessary.

Disciplinary Procedures

Employers must give employees details of any disciplinary rules applicable to them and the name of someone to whom appeal can be made against a disciplinary decision as part of the writtern particulars of the contract of employment. It should be emphasized that the law does not require organizations to have disciplinary rules or procedures. However, as we shall see, employers who act unfairly in disciplining employees are likely to face adverse tribunal decisions if dismissed employees seek legal redress. The ground rules on fairness are set out in the *Code of Practice on Disciplinary Practices and Procedures in Employment* issued by ACAS. Wise employers have incorporated the approaches to discipline recommended here into their own procedures and practices. Though infringements of the Code are not of themselves actionable offences, the absence of procedures or their breach is likely to make it difficult for the employer to argue that the action was fair before a tribunal. However, account will be taken of the size of the organization and the circumstances of the case.

The Essential Features of a Disciplinary Procedure

The Code of Practice says that disciplinary procedures should:

- be in writing
- specify to whom they apply
- provide for matters to be dealt with quickly
- indicate the disciplinary action which may be taken
- specify the levels of management which have the authority to take the various forms of disciplinary action, ensuring that immediate superiors do not normally have the power to dismiss without reference to senior management
- provide for indviduals to be informed of the complaints against them and to be given an opportunity to state their case before decisions are reached
- give individuals the right to be accompanied by a trade union representative or by a fellow employee of their choice

- ensure that, except for gross misconduct, no employees are dismissed for a first breach of discipline
- ensure that disciplinary action is not taken until the case has been carefully investigated
- ensure that individuals are given an explanation for any penalties imposed
- provide a right of appeal and specify the procedure to be followed.

The Code also suggests that if, after investigation, it is found that formal action should be taken against the employee the following stages should be followed:

- In the case of minor offences, the employee should be given a formal oral warning or, if the issue is more serious, there should be a written warning and the employee should be advised that the warning constitutes the first formal steps of the procedure
- Further misconduct might warrant a final written warning
- The final step might be disciplinary transfer or suspension without pay (but only if these are allowed for by an express or implied term of the contract of employment), or dismissal.

Trade Unions and Disciplinary Procedures

An important part of the trade union representative's role, where unions are recognized, is the representation of members subject to disciplinary action. *The Code of Practice* emphasizes the legitimacy of this. Many descriplinary procedures have been jointly agreed with trade unions which generally see them as a means of ensuring equitable treatment of employees. When it comes to disciplinary rules, trade unions are likely to be less willing to share control with management. Many trade unionists argue that it is vital to maintain flexibility here to protect members' interests.

Care should be taken if it becomes necessary to discipline a trade union representative, since this could be seen as an attack on the union. The *Code of Practice* suggests that no formal action should be taken until the matter has been discussed with either a full-time union official or with a more senior representative.

The Law on Dismissal

Observance of the guidance set out earlier in this section should be helpful in maintenance of good employee relations and supportive of the employer's case should subsequent dismissal lead to a tribunal hearing. To deal effectively with dismissal, managers and personnel specialists also need a good knowledge of the law. This is contained mainly within the Employment Protection Consolidation Act 1978, though there were minor amendments in the Employment Act 1980.

What Is Dismissal?

According to the law employees are treated as dismissed if:

- the contract of employment under which they work is terminated by the employer with or without notice
- a fixed term contract expires without being renewed
- they leave the job 'in circumstances such that (they are) entitled to terminate it without notice by reason of the employer's conduct' (constructive dismissal).

Constructive Dismissal

This occurs when management puts pressure on the employee to resign in a way which goes to the root of the contract. The most obvious example is where management materially changes the contract of employment without the employee's consent. For example, suppose the owner of a chain of five hairdressing salons tells a stylist that, in a month's time, she must transfer to another salon in the chain. Is this constructive dismissal? To decide this it would be necessary to examine the contract of employment and the effect on it of the employee's conduct. If the contract says that she has been employed as a stylist at any of the shops, and it is customary for staff to move around in this way, the employer may be in the clear. But if the contract states that the location of her employment is the salon in which she is currently working, she has worked there for a long time and stylists are never expected to move, the employer's case will be very weak. To make a claim of constructive dismissal, she must leave without notice. Management's best protection against such claims is to obtain her agreement to the move.

Who Can Claim Unfair Dismissal?

Employees with at least 2 years' service, who work more than 16 hours a week and part timers, who work more than 8 hours a week and have at least 5 years' continuous service, have the right to claim unfair dismissal. Employees who 'normally' work abroad, those over normal retirement age and those employed by a spouse are among those excluded from bringing unfair dismissal cases. If employees allege that their dismissal is due to trade union membership or activities or race or sex discrimination, they need not have the normal service qualification to bring the claim.

What Is Fair or Unfair Dismissal?

Once it has been established that a dismissal has taken place, the employer must prove that the employee was dismissed for one of the potentially fair reasons laid down in law. These are:

- lack of capability or qualifications for the work which the employee must do
- conduct
- redundancy
- where continuing to employ the worker would be illegal
- some other substantial reason.

However, showing that the employee was dismissed for a fair reason is not sufficient. The employer must also be able to prove that the punishment – the dismissal – fitted the crime.

If the employer fails to show the reason or shows a reason which is not listed above, the dismissal will be automatically unfair. If a valid reason is shown, the employer must show it was reasonable to dismiss the employee in the circumstances. Tribunals will pay careful attention to the facts of the particular case.

The law has different standards for small and large businesss. Small firms are treated more leniently, for example, for failing to use fair procedures or failing to offer alternative work to employees who become unable to cope with the demands of their jobs.

Now we shall examine the general approach of the courts and tribunals to dismissal under the five potentially valid reasons listed above.

Job Performance

This covers such matters as employee incompetence (intentional or unintentional), short and long term sickness and lack of qualifications to do the job.

If an employee falls below expected standards of performance, management must show that the reasons for the decline have been investigated, warnings have been given and attempts have been made to help the employee to improve. Whether or not it is necessary to offer alternative work will depend on the size of the organization and the length of service of the employee. Similar considerations will apply where employees' poor health makes them incapable of meeting the demands of their job. The law on dismissal due to long-term sickness is particularly complex. Obviously warnings that a failure to return to work will result in dismissal would be inappropriate. Employers are expected to be sympathetic and to hold open the job as long as is reasonably practicable. Tribunals will attempt to balance the employer's need for the work to be done against the employee's need to make a proper recovery.

In cases of short term absence from work, a different approach is appropriate. Here, warnings of the necessity to improve attendance should be given, though again the circumstances must be investigated. Medical certificates can be requested even for single days of absence. In making a decision to dismiss, it is quite legitimate to take into account the disruption of repeated short spells of absence on the efficiency of the organization.

The cases on lack of qualification are few since this must be a condition of the contract of employment. Most people who lack adequate qualifications are not selected in the first place. An example under this heading would be where a trainee fails to pass the examinations vital to practice the job. Even then, it might be reasonable for the employer to extend the training.

Conduct

This term is not defined in the legislation and an examination of cases indicates that a wide range of misconduct has been said to justify dismissal. Broadly, if an offence is accepted as gross misconduct, dismissal without notice would be appropriate. For less serious cases, it is vital that procedures are followed and that employees who breach disciplinary rules are treated equitably.

Redundancy

Employers must act reasonably in selecting employees for redundancy. The courts have laid down principles of good practice in these circumstances:

- as much warning as possible should be given of impending redundancies so that employers and unions together can seek alternative solutions or other work for those involved
- unions should be consulted so that management can achieve its objective with the minimum of hardship to those concerned
- criteria for selection should be objective and related to such things as attendance, experience, efficiency and length of service. Where possible, they should be agreed with trade unions
- selection should be on the basis of these criteria
- management should investigate the possibilities of alternative employment for those involved.

In addition, it would be unfair to select employees for redundancy on grounds of either trade union membership or non-membership.

Legal Restrictions

An employer may fairly dismiss an employee whose

continued employment would be against the law. This covers such cases as drivers who become disqualified from driving or those who do not have a work permit.

Some Other Substantial Reason

This last 'catch all' category has been used to cover such matters as reductions in wages or changes in hours of work which are argued by the employer to be vital if the business is to survive, dismissal of temporary employees who have been employed to replace staff absent because of medical suspension or maternity leave, and irreconcilable conflict between employees where the dismissed employee can be shown to be the main instigator of the trouble.

Reasons for Dismissal which are Automatically Unfair

These are:

- dismissal for being a member of or taking part in the activities of an independent trade union
- dismissal because of race or sex discrimination
- dismissal because of pregnancy unless the employer can show that the woman is no longer capable of doing the work she was employed to do

The dismissal of strikers is not automatically unfair provided none of them are re-engaged within six months of the dismissal. Neither is it automatically unfair to dismiss those who refuse to join a closed shop, though in this case there are major exceptions. (See *Pan Management Guide, Industrial Relations* by Chris Brewster, 1987).

Remedies for Unfair Dismissal

Employees who successfully bring a claim of unfair dismissal against their employer are entitled to remedies in this order:

- reinstatement
- re-engagement
- compensation.

Reinstatement

If the tribunal orders reinstatement, management must treat the employee as if the employment had not been terminated. That is management should take account of:

- back pay including any pay increase which should have been received
- the need to preserve the dismissed employee's continuity of service
- any benefits to which the dismissed employee is entitled – holiday pay, for example
- the date by which the tribunal's order for reinstatement is to be complied with.

Tribunals seldom order reinstatement. In making such decisions they take account of the employee's wishes, the practicality of such an order for management and the degree to which the employee contributed to the dismissal.

Re-engagement

In this case, the employee must be re-employed but not necessarily in the same job. Again, the cases in which tribunals make such an order are relatively small and the same factors are taken account of as for reinstatement.

Compensation

This is awarded if management is not ordered to re-employ the dismissed employee or if such an order is ignored.

There are four types of compensation:

- the basic award – equivalent to a redundancy payment
- the compensatory award – based on assessment of what the employee will lose in wages, benefits etc. now and in the future
- the additional award – if management do not comply with an order for reinstatement or reengagement
- the special award – in cases of dismissal for union membership or non-membership.

Both the basic award and the compensatory award will be reduced if the tribunal believes that the employee contributed to the dismissal. The compensatory award is reduced also if the employee failed to attempt to compensate for the loss of the job.

Dismissed workers are also entitled to a written statement of the reasons for their dismissal. If this has not been given, a tribunal can order additional compensation of up to two weeks' pay.

2 Redundancy

This is probably the saddest and most difficult aspect of employment relations with which managers and personnel specialists may have to deal; the issues involved include:

- Who to make redundant, in which areas of the business and on what date or dates?
- Would retraining of redundant employees be in

the interests of the organization?
- What compensation should be awarded to those made redundant?

Managers must think about these issues whatever the detailed circumstances. In unionized organizations it will also be vital to draw up a programme for consulting the unions. This may or may not involve the negotiation of a procedure for handling the redundancies, if such an agreement does not already exist. Sometimes management takes steps to assist redundant employees to find other work. Most often this occurs where the effect of the loss of jobs on the local community is likely to be severe. However, it is also sensible to consider those who will remain in work.

As explained in Chapter 9, employees with two years' service or more (five years for those working between eight and sixteen hours a week) can claim redundancy compensation. Workers must have been dismissed before they can make a claim. The legal definition of dismissal on p.147 applies to dismissals because of redundancy. Redundant workers may bring claims for unfair dismissal, as we saw on p.151. In this section we examine employees' rights to redundancy compensation as distinct from compensation for unfair dismissal.

Situations of Redundancy

The definition of redundancy covers three key situations:

- where the business ceases to operate
- where the employer changes the location of the business
- where the employer requires fewer employees for the existing work.

The first of these categories has created few problems in the courts.

If management wishes to move to another place, the

question as to whether workers are redundant will depend on the details of the contract of employment. If this does not require them to move, they will be able to claim redundancy compensation.

The most controversial redundancy cases have arisen where management decides that there is less work for employees to do or that the same work can be done by fewer people. In such cases, work may be reorganized and technology changed with consequent implications for the terms and conditions of employment under which people are employed. The courts have upheld management's right to reorganize work in the interests of efficiency. In doing so they have argued that redundancy arises only if there is a change in terms and conditions of employment because the employer's need for 'work of a particular kind' has 'ceased' or 'diminished'. Similarly, where the requirement for overtime is reduced, employees are not redundant if management still requires them to do their work as before.

Selection of Employees for Redundancy

The selection of those employees who must leave can be very painful. We looked at the legal restrictions on this in the last section. Very often, selection criteria are agreed with trade unions either at the time of redundancy or when redundancy is only a small dark cloud in an otherwise clear sky.

Redundancy is a difficult issue for trade unions. The views of the members are often divided; some will want to leave with the best possible compensation; others will feel the union should fight all job losses. However, as redundancy has become more common, trade union opposition has been reduced both by legal rights to compensation and to be consulted and by weakening of worker power as dole queues have lengthened. In unionized workplaces, there is likely to be a demand that volunteers should be allowed to go first. Acquiescence to this may have some disadvantages from management's point of view; those who volunteer are likely to include some people who would find it easy to get other jobs, people whose skills management would wish to retain.

By contrast, management may wish to make redundant those who make the smallest contribution to the efficiency of the organization – 'slackers', 'passengers', 'deadwood', etc. This is where many managers and personnel specialists face something of a crisis of conscience, for in all probability these people will be those who have the greatest difficulty in finding other jobs. In such situations 'last in first out' may seem to be a fairer criterion. Sometimes criteria are formalized in a redundancy procedure agreement, but often management is reluctant to restrict its flexibility to act in this way.

Legally, employers must CONSULT recognized independent unions about every proposed redundancy. All employees are covered apart from short-term workers employed for a period of three months or less. The law does not say that there must be negotiation with the unions. 'Consultation' involves giving, in writing, to the union:

- the reasons for the proposals of redundancy
- the numbers and description (i.e. jobs) of the employees
- the total number of employees in those jobs
- the proposed method of selecting employees for redundancy
- the proposed method of carrying out the redundancies – timing, methods of payment, etc.

After this, management must consider the union's views and must reply to them, stating the reasons for rejecting any of them.

The law says that consultation over any redundancies

must begin 'at the earliest opportunity'. When large numbers of redundancies are proposed, the following timetable must be observed at the minimum:

- If 100 employees are to be made redundant at one establishment over a period of up to ninety days, consultation must take place at least ninety days before the first dismissal takes place.
- If between 10 and 100 workers are to be made redundant at one establishment over a period of up to thirty days, consultation must take place at least thirty days before the first dismissal takes place.

If management does not observe this timetable, employees made redundant are entitled to additional compensation. This consists of payment for the 'protected period', i.e. the ninety or thirty days specified for the above categories. Tribunals reduce this amount by earnings or payments in lieu of notice paid during this period.

The Department of Employment also must be notified in writing using a similar timetable. Employers are entitled to a rebate from a national fund in respect of statutory redundancy payments. Failure to give the necessary notice to the Department of Employment can result in a reduction in rebate.

Retraining or Redevelopment of Redundant Workers

Retraining for work elsewhere can be an expensive option, especially when unemployment is high or where workers' skills are obsolete. Some organizations offer counselling services to redundant employees to demonstrate their concern, relieve anxieties and enhance the reputation of the organization as an employer in the long run.

The speed of technical change tends to mean that adaptation to the demands of new jobs will be a permanent feature of employment. The need for a flexible labour force should add emphasis to the need for planning to identify areas of redundant skills so that the viability of retraining can be thoroughly investigated.

It may be possible to offer some redundant employees new jobs immediately. In law if employees accept 'suitable alternative work' they are not entitled to redundancy compensation. For such offers of work to be suitable the following conditions must be met:

- the offer must be made before the old contract is terminated and must take effect within four weeks
- the offer must be made by the old employer, by management of the same group of companies or by a new employer who is taking over the business
- the offer can be made orally or in writing and must give the employee information about 'capacity and place . . . and . . . other terms and conditions of employment'
- sufficient information must be given to enable the employee to make a decision as to the suitability of the new job.

If the employee refuses alternative work which is suitable, the right to redundancy compensation is forfeited. In making decisons as to suitability, the tribunal takes account of the employee's personal circumstances including travel, housing, domestic problems or loss of friends.

Employees who are offered a new job have the right to try it for a period of four weeks. During this period they can leave at any time and claim redundancy compensation. It is then up to the tribunal to decide whether the new job was suitable and whether its rejection was reasonable.

Redundancy Compensation

Scales of minimum compensation in cases of redundancy are laid down by law. The amount of the payment depends on the employee's age, length of service and weekly pay. Only those who have two or more years' service have a legal entitlement to be compensated in this way. Many organizations have paid more to redundant workers than the statutory minimum. Employees have the right to a written statement from management explaining how the compensation has been calculated. Redundant workers also have the right to 'reasonable' paid time off to look for other work or for retraining whilst under notice of redundancy. This is only available to workers with at least two years' service. Even if employees are offered alternative work, they are entitled to this. There is no legal definition of what is reasonable. It would depend on the circumstances such as the amount of work available and the time and travel involved in looking for it. In practice the amount of time off tends to be rather limited. If management refuses to allow this right, the maximum compensation which can be awarded by a tribunal is two days.

Those Who Remain After Redundancy

The announcement of redundancy, especially if large numbers of people are involved, usually sends tremors throughout the organization. Those who stay may feel that their employment with the organization is no longer permanent and that their career prospects have been affected adversely. Management must systematically assess the nature of these changes and immediately should set about the rebuilding process in ways which convince remaining employees that they have a future.

3 Occupational Pension Schemes

This is a complex subject on which managers and personnel specialists require specialist advice from actuaries and investment advisers. Here we are only scratching the surface. Pensions are probably the most important employee benefit. There are many reasons why organizations seek to provide the best possible occupational pension scheme for employees. These include:

- to help the recruitment and retention of employees, especially more senior and older employees
- to demonstrate that the organization is a good employer; this should assist the commitment of employees
- to enable those who retire to enjoy financial security in their later years.

Contributory and Non-Contributory Occupational Pension Schemes

Most pension schemes require employees to contribute part of their earnings – usually six or seven per cent – to the fund from which they will later receive a pension. These are contributory schemes. In this sense pensions are a form of deferred earnings. Other schemes are non-contributory in that their full cost is paid by the employer.

Contributory schemes generally provide a better range of benefits because more money is available. Also, employees are often more appreciative of benefits for which they have paid.

By contrast, non-contributory schemes are often cheaper to administer, are flexible and very attractive to employees since no deductions are made from pay. Trade unions are generally not in favour of non-contributory schemes since they may act as 'golden chains' which tie employees to the organization because benefits are forfeited on leaving.

Who Is Covered?

It is common to find schemes which cover both staff and manual workers; however, senior management often have a 'top-hat' arrangement in which the scheme is topped up with a non-contributory arrangement.

Benefits

The most obvious benefit is a pension on retirement. Other benefits are:

- a lump sum on retirement
- death-in-service benefit
- pension for widows or widowers.

In addition, pension schemes can be more or less infla-tion proofed by allowing for increases in response to changes in the cost of living. This is a very desirable feature, although it can be expensive.

Provisions for Early Retirement

One way of avoiding compulsory redundancy is for employees nearing retirement age to retire early. Many organizations also allow employees in poor health to leave early. Pension schemes have to cope with this eventuality. Normally, such people can draw a pension immediately but, as their contributions will have been less than those who retire normally, their pension will be smaller. Some employers are generous in the pen-sions which are paid to older workers who retire at a time of redundancy. Lump sum payments may also be made. The early retirement option will not always be seen in such a rosy light. For management it is an expensive option because of the need to pay pensions early. In addition, it cannot always be assumed that older employees have outdated skills and knowledge. In many cases such people's years of experience are of value to the organization. Early retirement is usually voluntary. Thus management gives control of the selection process to employees. This may mean that the more useful older employees will leave while others whom management would wish to lose stay.

Provisions for Late Retirement

Sometimes employers want to retain the services of certain employees beyond retirement age. The rules of pension schemes usually provide for such people to receive an enhanced pension without further contributions either from them or from the employer.

In conclusion, it is dangerous to generalize about people. Not all older employees are ready to retire. To attempt to encourage all this group to leave before normal retirement age is a superficially simple way of coping with redundancy. Good personnel practice demands that the needs of both organization and individuals concerned must be carefully analysed before starting on this path.

Index

ACAS 40–1
action learning 95–6
added value 139
advertisements 21–3
application forms 21–3
assessment centres 80
autonomous work groups 58

canteens 105
career development 97–9
collective bargaining 61–2
Commission for Racial Equality 43, 111
conciliation 41–2
contract of employment 47–50
corporate planning 11–13
counselling 102–4

direct participation 55–6
Disabled Persons (Employment) Acts 43
disabled workers 47
disciplinary procedures 144–7
discipline 142–7
discrimination 43–7, 110–15
discrimination, direct 43
discrimination, indirect 44
discrimination, positive 111
discrimination, Sex Discrimination Act 43–6, 111
dismissal 147–154

education 74–5
employee handbooks 37–8
employee involvement 51–64
employee participation 55–63
employee services 100–7, 111
employment agencies 23

employment appeal tribunal 41–2
Equal Opportunities Commission 43, 111
equal opportunities policies 98–9, 110–111
equal pay 112–115
equal value 114
evaluation of management development 97
evaluation of recruitment and selection 34–5
evaluation of training 87–9
external pay comparisons 133–135

fringe benefits 100–7, 111

genuine occupational qualification 46
Goldthorpe J.H. 55
guarantee payments 118

halo effect 26–7
Herzberg F. 54
human resource planning 12–13, 92–3

indirect participation 60–3
induction 35–8
induction training 38–9
industrial democracy 61–3
industrial tribunals 41
interview structure 31
interviewer bias 26–7
interviewing, disciplinary 143–4
interviewing, selection 25–32

job analysis 18–19
job descriptions 19
job design 56–8
job enlargement 56, 57–8
job enrichment 57
job evaluation 114–5, 123–33
job rotation 56
joint consultation 61

labour, demand for 12, 92–3
labour, supply of 13, 92
labour, turnover 35

management coaching 96–7
management development 91–8
managerial prerogative 60
Maslow A. 52–4
maternity rights 115–16
measured daywork 138–9
medical screening 107
medical suspension 117–8
motivation 51–4

occupational health 106–7
orientation to work 55

panel interviews 31
pay levels 120
payment by results 137–40
pension schemes 161–3
performance appraisal 65–73
person specifications 19–21
personnel policies 10–11
personnel roles 14–16
profit sharing 139–40

quality circles 58–9
questioning techniques 27–30

Race Relations Act 43–6, 111
recruitment 16–23, 34–5, 45–6
redundancy 104–5, 151, 154–60
references 34
Rehabilitation of Offenders Act 1974 43
retirement 104, 161–3

salary surveys 133–5
selection 24–35, 45
selection testing 32–4, 80
self-managed learning 96
seven point plan 20–1
shortlisting 25
sick pay 117–8
sickness 105
single staff status 107
sports and social facilities 105–6
stress 107
stress interviews 30
succession planning 92–3
suggestion schemes 59–60

time off 116–7
trade union representatives 116–7
trade unions 116–7, 146–9
training 38–9, 74–99, 111
training needs analysis 77–9
training, on the job 82
training, systematic approach to 76–7
training, evaluation of 87–90
training, methods 85–6
training, objectives 74–6, 81
training, off the job 82
training, plans 78–9
training, policy 74–6

unfair dismissal 148–154

victimization 44–5

wage and salary policies 121–3
wage and salary, administration 135–6
wage-effort bargain 120–1
welfare 100–7
worker control 62–3
worker cooperatives 62–3
worker directors 62

young employees 97–8, 104

Mike Savedra and John Hawthorn
Supervision £2.95

a fresh approach

Supervision explains the key principles and functions of supervisory management: how to control, motivate and discipline people, how to plan, organize and assess work, how to communicate information. The authors draw on examples and case studies from industry, public services, government, education and the forces throughout a comprehensive treatment.

Roger Oldcorn
Management £3.95

a fresh approach

A fresh introduction to the role of the modern manager. Coverage is geared to various syllabus requirements including the CNAA Diploma in Management Studies and those of the Institute of Industrial Management, Institute of Personnel Management, Institute of Purchasing and Supply and BEC Certificate in Management Studies courses.

A Pan Breakthrough book, published in collaboration with the National Extension College.

Nicki Stanton
What Do You Mean, 'Communication'? £3.95
an introduction to communication in business

Describes the scope, skills and techniques of business communication. Coverage is geared especially to communications courses at BEC National and Higher levels whilst serving various other syllabus requirements: RSA Stage II, LCCI Intermediate, City & Guilds Communication Skills, and foundation courses for professional examinations.

A Pan Breakthrough book, published in collaboration with the National Extension College.

The Business of Communicating £3.95
improving your communicating skills

Advice on the key elements of communication: writing letters, using the phone, interviewing, speaking in public. This book develops the principles explained in *What Do You Mean, 'Communication'?*. Coverage is geared to communication courses at BEC National and Higher levels whilst serving various other syllabus requirements: RSA Stage II, LCCI Intermediate, City & Guilds Communication Skills, foundation courses for professional examinations.

A Pan Breakthrough book, published in collaboration with the National Extension College.

Chris Brewster
Understanding Industrial Relations £2.95

Emphasizes the importance of management's role before explaining
the involvement of unions and the state. The legal framework is shown
in detail and later chapters examine industrial relations in practice, at the
workplace and during negotiations. Ideal for use on Institute of
Industrial Management, Institute of Personnel Management and
NEBSS courses and for practising managers.

A Pan Breakthrough book, published in collaboration with the National
Extension College.

Rita Harris
Understanding Office Practice £2.95

Explains and illustrates the structure and working methods of the
modern office, covering all the traditional skills and devoting close
attention to the impact of new technology. The book caters for many
syllabuses and training courses: BEC General Level World of Work,
Office Machines and Equipment, Clerical Services; MSC Youth Training
Schemes; SCOTBEC, RSA and LCCI Office Practice.

A Pan Breakthrough book, published in collaboration with the National
Extension College.

Peter F. Drucker
Management   £3.95

Peter Drucker's aim in this major book is 'to prepare today's and
tomorrow's managers for performance'. He presents his philosophy of
management, refined as a craft with specific skills: decision making,
communication, control and measurement, analysis – skills essential for
effective and responsible management in the late twentieth century.

'Crisp, often arresting . . . A host of stories and case histories from Sears
Roebuck, Marks and Spencer, IBM, Siemens, Mitsubishi and other
modern giants lend colour and credibility to the points he makes'
ECONOMIST

Managing for Results   £2.95

'A guide to do-it-yourself management . . . contains first-class
suggestions that have the great virtue that they are likely to be widely
and easily applicable to almost every business'
TIMES REVIEW OF INDUSTRY

'Excellent . . . well-supported examples of what has happened in
practice to companies that have thought in this analytical way'
FINANCIAL TIMES

Derek French and Heather Saward
Dictionary of Management   £4.95

A handy reference work providing definitions for nearly 4000 terms, abbreviations and techniques current in general and functional management and in such areas as government, law and economics that affect the manager's work. An indispensable source of information for managers, students and interested laymen who wish to extend their understanding of the modern business world.

John Hunt
Managing People at Work   £3.50

Here, at last, is a lucid analysis of recent developments in sociology and psychology and their implications for managers. John Hunt presents, in a readable form, relevant ideas from the major areas of organizational behaviour: motivation, perception, communication, groups, roles, power, organizations, structures, managers, leaders, participation and change. His objective is to let managers decide for themselves whether behavioural tools can be useful and valuable to them.

John Adair
Effective Leadership £2.95

a modern guide to developing leadership skills

The art of leadership demands a keen ability to appraise, understand and inspire both colleagues and subordinates. In this unique guide, John Adair, Britain's foremost expert on leadership training, shows how every manager can learn to lead. He draws upon numerous illustrations of leadership in action – commercial, historical and military – to pinpoint the essential requirements.

Effective Decision-Making £2.95

Few managers devote enough attention to the *thinking* processes they should apply to their jobs. Yet long, energetic hours at work are wasted if business decisions are not logical, clear and correct. *Effective Decision-Making* is the definitive guide to the crucial managerial skill of creative *thinking*. John Adair draws on examples and case studies from business, recent history, sport and entertainment in showing how to sharpen analytical management skills.

Katherine Aschner
The Word Processing Handbook £2.95

Word processors have revolutionized office life in the 1980s. Everyone involved in office life needs to understand how they operate and what they can do. This handbook takes readers step-by-step through word processing techniques and terminology, and, accompanied by numerous illustrations, answer most of the key questions involved.

Jacquetta Megarry
Computers Mean Business £3.95

Computers Mean Business uses simple language, clear illustrations and a comprehensive glossary to show how computers can increase profitability and efficiency. Jacquetta Megarry demonstrates the key business applications of computers, including data base management, accounting, stock control and word processing. She gives expert advice on choosing hardware and software, explains the fundamentals of programming and considers the special needs of the self-employed.

Rosemary Stewart
The Reality of Management £3.95

This book is addressed to all managers who want to improve their job effectiveness. It is also a definitive student's guide to management theory and practice. The emphasis is firmly on the areas of greatest current importance in management:

* decision-making
* leadership and development
* management and social climate
* managers and change

The whole work is updated to strengthen the advice it supplies to the managers of the eighties, and is complemented by the author's other book, *The Reality of Organization*. Together they represent the ideal introduction to a vitally important profession.

All these books are available at your local bookshop or newsagent, or can be ordered direct from the publisher. Indicate the number of copies required and fill in the form below   12

....

Name_____
(Block letters please)

Address_____

_____

Send to CS Department, Pan Books Ltd,
PO Box 40, Basingstoke, Hants
Please enclose remittance to the value of the cover price plus:
35p for the first book plus 15p per copy for each additional book ordered
to a maximum charge of £1.25 to cover postage and packing
Applicable only in the UK

While every effort is made to keep prices low, it is sometimes necessary to increase prices at short notice. Pan Books reserve the right to show on covers and charge new retail prices which may differ from those advertised in the text or elsewhere